YASIR ARAFAT

YASIR ARAFAT

Rebecca Stefoff

CHELSEA HOUSE PUBLISHERS
NEW YORK
PHILADELPHIA

Chelsea House Publishers
EDITOR-IN-CHIEF: Nancy Toff
EXECUTIVE EDITOR: Remmel T. Nunn
MANAGING EDITOR: Karyn Gullen Browne
COPY CHIEF: Juliann Barbato
PICTURE EDITOR: Adrian G. Allen
ART DIRECTOR: Giannella Garrett
MANUFACTURING MANAGER: Gerald Levine

World Leaders—Past & Present
SENIOR EDITOR: John W. Selfridge

Staff for YASIR ARAFAT:
ASSISTANT EDITOR: Sean Dolan
COPY EDITORS: Terrance Dolan, Karen Hammonds
DEPUTY COPY CHIEF: Ellen Scordato
EDITORIAL ASSISTANT: Sean Ginty
PICTURE RESEARCHER: Lynne Goldberg
DESIGNER: Ghila Krajzman
PRODUCTION COORDINATOR: Joseph Romano
COVER ILLUSTRATION: Alan Nahigian

3 5 7 9 8 6 4

Library of Congress Cataloging in Publication Data

Stefoff, Rebecca.
Yasir Arafat.

(World leaders past & present)
Bibliography: p.
Includes index.
Summary: A biography of the man who since 1969 has been chairman of
the Palestine Liberation Organization, a group working to establish an
Arab state in what was once Palestine and is now mostly in Israel.
1. Arafat, Yasir, 1929–. —Juvenile literature.
2. Palestinian Arabs—Biography—Juvenile
literature.   3. Jewish-Arab relations—1949– —Juvenile
literature.   4. Munazzamat al-Tahrīr al-Filastīnīyah—
Juvenile literature.   5. Israel-Arab conflicts—Juvenile
literature.   [1. Arafat, Yasir, 1929– . 2. Palestinian
Arabs—Biography] I. Title. II. Series.
DS119.7.S674   1988   322.4′2′0924 [B] [92] 87-32564

ISBN 1-55546-826-8
    0-7910-0591-7 (pbk.)

Contents

JOHN ADAMS
JOHN QUINCY ADAMS
KONRAD ADENAUER
ALEXANDER THE GREAT
SALVADOR ALLENDE
MARC ANTONY
CORAZON AQUINO
YASIR ARAFAT
KING ARTHUR
HAFEZ AL-ASSAD
KEMAL ATATÜRK
ATTILA
CLEMENT ATTLEE
AUGUSTUS CAESAR
MENACHEM BEGIN
DAVID BEN-GURION
OTTO VON BISMARCK
LÉON BLUM
SIMON BOLÍVAR
CESARE BORGIA
WILLY BRANDT
LEONID BREZHNEV
JULIUS CAESAR
JOHN CALVIN
JIMMY CARTER
FIDEL CASTRO
CATHERINE THE GREAT
CHARLEMAGNE
CHIANG KAI-SHEK
WINSTON CHURCHILL
GEORGES CLEMENCEAU
CLEOPATRA
CONSTANTINE THE GREAT
HERNÁN CORTÉS
OLIVER CROMWELL
GEORGES-JACQUES
  DANTON
JEFFERSON DAVIS
MOSHE DAYAN
CHARLES DE GAULLE
EAMON DE VALERA
EUGENE DEBS
DENG XIAOPING
BENJAMIN DISRAELI
ALEXANDER DUBČEK
FRANÇOIS & JEAN-CLAUDE
  DUVALIER
DWIGHT EISENHOWER
ELEANOR OF AQUITAINE
ELIZABETH I
FAISAL
FERDINAND & ISABELLA
FRANCISCO FRANCO
BENJAMIN FRANKLIN

FREDERICK THE GREAT
INDIRA GANDHI
MOHANDAS GANDHI
GIUSEPPE GARIBALDI
AMIN & BASHIR GEMAYEL
GENGHIS KHAN
WILLIAM GLADSTONE
MIKHAIL GORBACHEV
ULYSSES S. GRANT
ERNESTO "CHE" GUEVARA
TENZIN GYATSO
ALEXANDER HAMILTON
DAG HAMMARSKJÖLD
HENRY VIII
HENRY OF NAVARRE
PAUL VON HINDENBURG
HIROHITO
ADOLF HITLER
HO CHI MINH
KING HUSSEIN
IVAN THE TERRIBLE
ANDREW JACKSON
JAMES I
WOJCIECH JARUZELSKI
THOMAS JEFFERSON
JOAN OF ARC
POPE JOHN XXIII
POPE JOHN PAUL II
LYNDON JOHNSON
BENITO JUÁREZ
JOHN KENNEDY
ROBERT KENNEDY
JOMO KENYATTA
AYATOLLAH KHOMEINI
NIKITA KHRUSHCHEV
KIM IL SUNG
MARTIN LUTHER KING, JR.
HENRY KISSINGER
KUBLAI KHAN
LAFAYETTE
ROBERT E. LEE
VLADIMIR LENIN
ABRAHAM LINCOLN
DAVID LLOYD GEORGE
LOUIS XIV
MARTIN LUTHER
JUDAS MACCABEUS
JAMES MADISON
NELSON & WINNIE
  MANDELA
MAO ZEDONG
FERDINAND MARCOS
GEORGE MARSHALL

MARY, QUEEN OF SCOTS
TOMÁS MASARYK
GOLDA MEIR
KLEMENS VON METTERNICH
JAMES MONROE
HOSNI MUBARAK
ROBERT MUGABE
BENITO MUSSOLINI
NAPOLÉON BONAPARTE
GAMAL ABDEL NASSER
JAWAHARLAL NEHRU
NERO
NICHOLAS II
RICHARD NIXON
KWAME NKRUMAH
DANIEL ORTEGA
MOHAMMED REZA PAHLAVI
THOMAS PAINE
CHARLES STEWART
  PARNELL
PERICLES
JUAN PERÓN
PETER THE GREAT
POL POT
MUAMMAR EL-QADDAFI
RONALD REAGAN
CARDINAL RICHELIEU
MAXIMILIEN ROBESPIERRE
ELEANOR ROOSEVELT
FRANKLIN ROOSEVELT
THEODORE ROOSEVELT
ANWAR SADAT
HAILE SELASSIE
PRINCE SIHANOUK
JAN SMUTS
JOSEPH STALIN
SUKARNO
SUN YAT-SEN
TAMERLANE
MOTHER TERESA
MARGARET THATCHER
JOSIP BROZ TITO
TOUSSAINT L'OUVERTURE
LEON TROTSKY
PIERRE TRUDEAU
HARRY TRUMAN
QUEEN VICTORIA
LECH WALESA
GEORGE WASHINGTON
CHAIM WEIZMANN
WOODROW WILSON
XERXES
EMILIANO ZAPATA
ZHOU ENLAI

CHELSEA HOUSE PUBLISHERS

ON LEADERSHIP

Arthur M. Schlesinger, jr.

LEADERSHIP, it may be said, is really what makes the world go round. Love no doubt smooths the passage; but love is a private transaction between consenting adults. Leadership is a public transaction with history. The idea of leadership affirms the capacity of individuals to move, inspire, and mobilize masses of people so that they act together in pursuit of an end. Sometimes leadership serves good purposes, sometimes bad; but whether the end is benign or evil, great leaders are those men and women who leave their personal stamp on history.

Now, the very concept of leadership implies the proposition that individuals can make a difference. This proposition has never been universally accepted. From classical times to the present day, eminent thinkers have regarded individuals as no more than the agents and pawns of larger forces, whether the gods and goddesses of the ancient world or, in the modern era, race, class, nation, the dialectic, the will of the people, the spirit of the times, history itself. Against such forces, the individual dwindles into insignificance.

So contends the thesis of historical determinism. Tolstoy's great novel *War and Peace* offers a famous statement of the case. Why, Tolstoy asked, did millions of men in the Napoleonic Wars, denying their human feelings and their common sense, move back and forth across Europe slaughtering their fellows? "The war," Tolstoy answered, "was bound to happen simply because it was bound to happen." All prior history predetermined it. As for leaders, they, Tolstoy said, "are but the labels that serve to give a name to an end and, like labels, they have the least possible connection with the event." The greater the leader, "the more conspicuous the inevitability and the predestination of every act he commits." The leader, said Tolstoy, is "the slave of history."

Determinism takes many forms. Marxism is the determinism of class. Nazism the determinism of race. But the idea of men and women as the slaves of history runs athwart the deepest human instincts. Rigid determinism abolishes the idea of human freedom—

the assumption of free choice that underlies every move we make, every word we speak, every thought we think. It abolishes the idea of human responsibility, since it is manifestly unfair to reward or punish people for actions that are by definition beyond their control. No one can live consistently by any deterministic creed. The Marxist states prove this themselves by their extreme susceptibility to the cult of leadership.

More than that, history refutes the idea that individuals make no difference. In December 1931 a British politician crossing Park Avenue in New York City between 76th and 77th Streets around 10:30 P.M. looked in the wrong direction and was knocked down by an automobile—a moment, he later recalled, of a man aghast, a world aglare: "I do not understand why I was not broken like an eggshell or squashed like a gooseberry." Fourteen months later an American politician, sitting in an open car in Miami, Florida, was fired on by an assassin; the man beside him was hit. Those who believe that individuals make no difference to history might well ponder whether the next two decades would have been the same had Mario Constasino's car killed Winston Churchill in 1931 and Giuseppe Zangara's bullet killed Franklin Roosevelt in 1933. Suppose, in addition, that Adolf Hitler had been killed in the street fighting during the Munich *Putsch* of 1923 and that Lenin had died of typhus during World War I. What would the 20th century be like now?

For better or for worse, individuals do make a difference. "The notion that a people can run itself and its affairs anonymously," wrote the philosopher William James, "is now well known to be the silliest of absurdities. Mankind does nothing save through initiatives on the part of inventors, great or small, and imitation by the rest of us—these are the sole factors in human progress. Individuals of genius show the way, and set the patterns, which common people then adopt and follow."

Leadership, James suggests, means leadership in thought as well as in action. In the long run, leaders in thought may well make the greater difference to the world. But, as Woodrow Wilson once said, "Those only are leaders of men, in the general eye, who lead in action. . . . It is at their hands that new thought gets its translation into the crude language of deeds." Leaders in thought often invent in solitude and obscurity, leaving to later generations the tasks of imitation. Leaders in action—the leaders portrayed in this series—have to be effective in their own time.

And they cannot be effective by themselves. They must act in response to the rhythms of their age. Their genius must be adapted, in a phrase of William James's, "to the receptivities of the moment." Leaders are useless without followers. "There goes the mob," said the French politician hearing a clamor in the streets. "I am their leader. I must follow them." Great leaders turn the inchoate emotions of the mob to purposes of their own. They seize on the opportunities of their time, the hopes, fears, frustrations, crises, potentialities. They succeed when events have prepared the way for them, when the community is awaiting to be aroused, when they can provide the clarifying and organizing ideas. Leadership ignites the circuit between the individual and the mass and thereby alters history.

It may alter history for better or for worse. Leaders have been responsible for the most extravagant follies and most monstrous crimes that have beset suffering humanity. They have also been vital in such gains as humanity has made in individual freedom, religious and racial tolerance, social justice, and respect for human rights.

There is no sure way to tell in advance who is going to lead for good and who for evil. But a glance at the gallery of men and women in *World Leaders—Past and Present* suggests some useful tests.

One test is this: Do leaders lead by force or by persuasion? By command or by consent? Through most of history leadership was exercised by the divine right of authority. The duty of followers was to defer and to obey. "Theirs not to reason why / Theirs but to do and die." On occasion, as with the so-called enlightened despots of the 18th century in Europe, absolutist leadership was animated by humane purposes. More often, absolutism nourished the passion for domination, land, gold, and conquest and resulted in tyranny.

The great revolution of modern times has been the revolution of equality. The idea that all people should be equal in their legal condition has undermined the old structure of authority, hierarchy, and deference. The revolution of equality has had two contrary effects on the nature of leadership. For equality, as Alexis de Tocqueville pointed out in his great study *Democracy in America*, might mean equality in servitude as well as equality in freedom.

"I know of only two methods of establishing equality in the political world," Tocqueville wrote. "Rights must be given to every citizen, or none at all to anyone . . . save one, who is the master of all." There was no middle ground "between the sovereignty of all and the absolute power of one man." In his astonishing prediction of 20th-century totalitarian dictatorship, Tocqueville explained how the revolution of equality could lead to the *"Führerprinzip"* and more terrible absolutism than the world had ever known.

But when rights are given to every citizen and the sovereignty of all is established, the problem of leadership takes a new form, becomes more exacting than ever before. It is easy to issue commands and enforce them by the rope and the stake, the concentration camp and the *gulag.* It is much harder to use argument and achievement to overcome opposition and win consent. The Founding Fathers of the United States understood the difficulty. They believed that history had given them the opportunity to decide, as Alexander Hamilton wrote in the first Federalist Paper, whether men are indeed capable of basing government on "reflection and choice, or whether they are forever destined to depend . . . on accident and force."

Government by reflection and choice called for a new style of leadership and a new quality of followership. It required leaders to be responsive to popular concerns, and it required followers to be active and informed participants in the process. Democracy does not eliminate emotion from politics; sometimes it fosters demagoguery; but it is confident that, as the greatest of democratic leaders put it, you cannot fool all of the people all of the time. It measures leadership by results and retires those who overreach or falter or fail.

It is true that in the long run despots are measured by results too. But they can postpone the day of judgment, sometimes indefinitely, and in the meantime they can do infinite harm. It is also true that democracy is no guarantee of virtue and intelligence in government, for the voice of the people is not necessarily the voice of God. But democracy, by assuring the right of opposition, offers built-in resistance to the evils inherent in absolutism. As the theologian Reinhold Niebuhr summed it up, "Man's capacity for justice makes democracy possible, but man's inclination to injustice makes democracy necessary."

A second test for leadership is the end for which power is sought. When leaders have as their goal the supremacy of a master race or the promotion of totalitarian revolution or the acquisition and exploitation of colonies or the protection of greed and privilege or the preservation of personal power, it is likely that their leadership will do little to advance the cause of humanity. When their goal is the abolition of slavery, the liberation of women, the enlargement of opportunity for the poor and powerless, the extension of equal rights to racial minorities, the defense of the freedoms of expression and opposition, it is likely that their leadership will increase the sum of human liberty and welfare.

Leaders have done great harm to the world. They have also conferred great benefits. You will find both sorts in this series. Even "good" leaders must be regarded with a certain wariness. Leaders are not demigods; they put on their trousers one leg after another just like ordinary mortals. No leader is infallible, and every leader needs to be reminded of this at regular intervals. Irreverence irritates leaders but is their salvation. Unquestioning submission corrupts leaders and demeans followers. Making a cult of a leader is always a mistake. Fortunately hero worship generates its own antidote. "Every hero," said Emerson, "becomes a bore at last."

The signal benefit the great leaders confer is to embolden the rest of us to live according to our own best selves, to be active, insistent, and resolute in affirming our own sense of things. For great leaders attest to the reality of human freedom against the supposed inevitabilities of history. And they attest to the wisdom and power that may lie within the most unlikely of us, which is why Abraham Lincoln remains the supreme example of great leadership. A great leader, said Emerson, exhibits new possibilities to all humanity. "We feed on genius. . . . Great men exist that there may be greater men."

Great leaders, in short, justify themselves by emancipating and empowering their followers. So humanity struggles to master its destiny, remembering with Alexis de Tocqueville: "It is true that around every man a fatal circle is traced beyond which he cannot pass; but within the wide verge of that circle he is powerful and free; as it is with man, so with communities."

1

Karameh

In March 1968 a day-long battle in an obscure village in the Middle Eastern kingdom of Jordan helped change the course of modern history. The fighting at Karameh involved small forces and claimed few lives, yet it was the springboard to power of a man who would become one of the most controversial world leaders of the late 20th century.

At Karameh, Yasir Arafat led a band of fewer than 300 Palestinian guerrilla fighters, many of them old men or children, against the attacking tanks and paratroops of the powerful Israeli army. Before the battle Arafat's supporters urged him to flee, arguing that resistance to the Israelis would lead only to his death or capture. But Arafat remained, and his stubborn courage made him a new hero to the Arabs and the leader of the Palestinian people.

He did not cut a heroic figure. At 38 he was short, pudgy, and rarely seen without a stubble of beard. By profession he was a civil engineer, but his customary uniform was a rumpled set of military fatigues, dark glasses to protect his weak eyes, and a combat cap or *kaffiyeh*, the traditional Arab headdress of checkered white cloth. He had worked for more than a decade, without much success, to turn

After the Arab defeat of 1967, there must be some group to give an example to the Arab nation—there must be some group who can prove that there are people in our Arab nation who are ready to fight and die
—YASIR ARAFAT

Yasir Arafat consults with a fellow member of al-Fatah, which he founded in the late 1950s. Under Arafat's leadership Fatah became the most important Palestinian liberation group. In 1969 Arafat was elected chairman of the Palestinian Liberation Organization (PLO).

scattered groups of anti-Israel guerrilla fighters into a unified revolutionary movement of international importance. Although something less than an outright victory, the battle of Karameh enabled him to accomplish this goal.

Karameh is located north of the Dead Sea, 25 miles west of the Jordanian capital of Amman, just a few miles east of the Jordan River. Much of the territory on the river's west bank was seized by Israel during its 1967 war with the neighboring Arab states of Jordan, Egypt, and Syria. (The West Bank and all of present-day Israel were called Palestine before the state of Israel was established in 1948.) The West Bank had been inhabited mainly by Palestinian Arabs. By 1968 Karameh was not an ordinary Jordanian peasant village but a refugee camp for the hundreds of Palestinians who had fled from the fighting on the West Bank or been displaced earlier by the creation of Israel. Among the refugees were members of a secret group of Palestinian guerrilla fighters called *al-Fatah*, or simply *Fatah*.

Fatah's soldiers were called *fedayeen*, an Arabic word that means both "men of sacrifice" and "commandos." Believing their homeland in Palestine had been stolen from them, the fedayeen dedicated themselves to war against the nation of Israel. They

On March 21, 1968, the Israeli Defense Forces (IDF) sent tanks and a large number of troops into Jordan to destroy a Fatah base in the village of Karameh. Although the fighting was a standoff, the battle was hailed in the Arab world as a great victory for Fatah.

used Karameh and other Jordanian villages as bases from which to launch lightning raids against people and property in Israel and on the West Bank, with the goal of winning back part or all of Palestine. In February 1968 Karameh became the headquarters of Yasir Arafat, Fatah's founder and military leader.

Arafat set up his headquarters in Karameh — the name means "dignity" in Arabic — because he was moved by the spirit of resistance shown by the Palestinian refugees there. King Hussein of Jordan was afraid that Israel would declare war against his nation if guerrilla attacks against Israel from bases in Jordan were allowed to continue and sent Jordanian soldiers to Karameh and other Palestinian settlements to arrest the fedayeen.

The refugees, however, did not believe that Hussein was willing or able to protect the unarmed settlements from Israeli attack. The previous November, Israeli mortar and fragmentation bombs had fallen on Karameh's police post, food distribution center, and girls' school, killing a number of Palestinians. Believing that Fatah was their only protection against further attacks, the refugees refused to turn over the fedayeen to the Jordanians. Instead, they surrounded the soldiers, shouting "Give us our fighters." The Jordanians left without making any arrests. Arafat arrived soon after and made Karameh into Fatah's chief base in Jordan.

Fatah's attacks against Israel usually took the form of stealthy sabotage. The fedayeen sneaked across the border and planted bombs and mines in Israeli territory. Sometimes the targets were electrical power stations, military posts, or irrigation pumps, but at other times civilians were killed or injured. On March 8 a Fatah mine damaged an Israeli school bus. A doctor was killed, and several children were badly hurt. Israel decided it was time to destroy the Fatah strongholds in Jordan — especially Karameh.

Within a few hours, Israeli tanks and troops were massing in the West Bank city of Jericho. Hussein was informed that the Israeli incursion would be directed only at the Palestinian bases, not at the

> *The people of the camp had ceased to believe that Jordan's armed forces could or would protect them; they had come to look upon the fedayeen as their only protectors.*
> —ALAN HART
> English historian and biographer, on Fatah's support at Karameh

Arafat meets with *fedayeen* (guerrilla fighters) in the mid-1960s. Intelligent and charismatic, Arafat won the support of many Palestinians for his leadership of Fatah.

Jordanian nation. Many Palestinians warned Arafat of the coming attack. Sympathetic Jordanian army officers told the fedayeen that the Israelis were boasting that they would soon parade captured Palestinian terrorist leaders down the streets of Jerusalem.

The Israelis had reason to be confident. Since the founding of their nation in 1948, they had defeated Arab armies in three separate wars and greatly expanded their nation's original territory. It did not seem that a few bands of guerrillas could present much of a threat to the vaunted Israeli Defense Force (IDF).

On March 20, as the Israelis prepared their attack, an Iraqi army officer who was stationed in Jordan reminded Arafat of the first rule of guerrilla warfare: A guerrilla force cannot stand and fight a much larger, better-equipped regular army. The officer of-

fered his troops to cover Arafat's retreat. To his astonishment, Arafat replied, "We will not withdraw. We will fight and we will die."

Why did Arafat decide to defend Karameh? At the time, he said he wanted to show the Arab people, Israel, and the world that the Palestinians were not afraid to die for their cause. Arafat felt that many Palestinian Arab leaders were ready to give up their fight against Israel, and he wanted to keep the struggle alive. He may also have hoped other nations would criticize Israel for invading Jordan and wiping out villages and innocent refugees.

Whatever his reasons, Arafat did not have much time to prepare his small force — 297 men — for the defense of Karameh. As the evening of the 20th fell, he called them together and urged them to face the Israeli attackers with courage. "We cannot defeat them," he said, "but we can teach them a lesson."

This Palestinian refugee camp outside Jordan's capital, Amman, was one of many founded in Jordan, Syria, and Lebanon after the establishment of the independent state of Israel in 1948. Hundreds of thousands of Palestinians fled or were driven from their homes following the creation of Israel.

The Jordanian soldiers had been positioned in the hills around Karameh. Their orders were to keep the Israeli forces from moving farther into Jordan and not to interfere in the fighting between the Israelis and the Palestinians.

The night passed slowly, and in the dark hour just before dawn the Israelis struck. Troop carriers and tanks rumbled across the Jordan River on the Allenby Bridge, just north of the Dead Sea, and headed for Karameh. Jet fighters streaked from airfields in Israel to circle over the Fatah bases. Protected by the jets, helicopters landed paratroops east of the village. The Israelis moved in from both sides — tanks from the west and paratroops from the east — and surrounded the village without a shot being fired. Karameh looked like a ghost town to the advancing Israelis. Not a single Palestinian could be seen.

For a few moments, the Israelis wondered what had gone wrong with their plan. Had the fedayeen slipped away under cover of darkness? Soldiers with loudspeakers ordered the inhabitants to come out of their houses with their hands up, but nothing happened. The Israeli tanks rolled into the central square—and then Arafat's counterattack began.

Fatah fighters emerged from holes in the ground and out of doorways. Some climbed onto the tanks and shoved grenades into their treads or gun muzzles. Others, with sticks of dynamite strapped to their bodies, threw themselves at the tanks as human bombs. Taken by surprise, Israeli soldiers jumped out of the crippled tanks and ran for cover. Although some fedayeen were killed in the counterattack, Fatah had the vaunted IDF on the run.

The Israelis soon regrouped and began to gain ground. By 11 A.M. the Israelis had once again advanced into the village, and about one-third of the Palestinians had been killed. It was difficult to see; the air was filled with great clouds of dust from the impact of grenades or shells upon the dry ground or the mud-brick walls of the village's huts. The distant booming of rocket launchers, the sudden, sharp rattle of rifle fire, the low roar of the tanks, and the screams of stricken fighters on both sides enveloped the village.

The IDF continued to advance, and it appeared as if the fedayeen would be defeated, but the Jordanian army, watching from the heights east of Karameh, opened fire on the Israelis. The IDF was now under attack from two sides.

Israeli troops scramble for cover during an attack by Egyptian MIG fighter planes during the Six-Day War of June 1967. It took the Israeli military less than a week to defeat the combined forces of Jordan, Syria, and Egypt.

Israeli soldiers assist an elderly Palestinian across the Allenby Bridge, which spans the Jordan River. Israel's victory in the Six-Day War enabled the nation to triple its size. More than a million Palestinians were displaced or came under Israeli military occupation.

Under cover of the Jordanian artillery barrage, Arafat and his fighters withdrew to new positions in the fields around Karameh, where they were joined by Fatah members newly arrived from Damascus, the capital of Syria. These fresh fighters carried antitank weapons and rocket-propelled grenades. Armed with this new equipment, small groups of Palestinians darted behind the Israeli lines to strike at tanks and armored cars.

By midafternoon the Israeli forces were pulling back across the Jordan River, and Arafat was on a motorcycle heading north toward shelter in the village of Salt. Israel claimed that it had successfully retaliated for recent terrorist acts by the Palestinians — official Israeli sources said that the IDF killed or captured more than 300 Palestinians and lost only 28 men, 6 tanks, and 2 armored cars — but Fatah and most outside observers claimed that the battle had really been Israel's first defeat at the hands of an Arab force. According to the Palestinians, Fatah lost only 93 fighters and captured or destroyed 18 IDF tanks.

Approximately 40 Jordanian soldiers were killed in the fighting around Karameh. If the Jordanians had not entered the battle, Fatah would probably have lost, and Arafat would most likely have been killed or captured. No one is certain why the Jordanians did join the battle. It has been suggested that Arafat or one of his lieutenants secretly made a deal with the Jordanians in advance, making sure of their support at a critical point in the battle. It is also possible that Jordan's King Hussein, who had been criticized by Arab and Palestinian leaders in the past for his ties to Great Britain and the United States and his insufficient commitment to the Palestinian cause and Arab nationalism, viewed the Israeli incursion as an opportunity to demonstrate his militancy to the rest of the Arab world. Many Palestinians believed simply that the Jordanians, their fellow Arabs, were inspired to disobey their orders when they saw the brave defense put up by Fatah.

Although today Karameh seems like a minor episode in the bloody history of the Israelis and the

Arabs in the Middle East, it was a turning point because it brought Yasir Arafat to the forefront of the Palestinian struggle. Some 40 years after Israel's creation, the Middle East continues to be one of the world's most volatile areas. With the exception of Egypt, the Arab nations continue to deny Israel's right to exist, while Israel, bolstered by aid from the United States, fields the strongest military in the region. Another generation of Palestinians — in some cases the grandchildren of those dispossessed in 1948 — has been born and raised in the refugee camps and villages of Lebanon and the West Bank and continues the fight against Israel. Despite manifold setbacks, Arafat continues as the most visible leader of the Palestinians, and he remains the individual most readily identified with their cause.

At Karameh, Arafat demonstrated the qualities that would enable him to master the volatile politics of the Arab world and endure as the leader of the Palestine liberation movement. Foremost among

Israeli troops distribute bread in the West Bank town of Qalqiyah shortly after the Israeli army secured its control over the area in June 1967. Although there was not an orchestrated campaign to drive the Palestinians from their homes, as there was in 1947–48, many fled to Jordan and other Arab states.

An Israeli patrol moves through the West Bank town of Nablus in 1969, two years after Israel took control of the region. Like other Palestinian towns and villages on the West Bank, Nablus became a center of support for the Palestine liberation movement.

them is what the Arabs call *baraka* — a divine blessing of good luck and power. His associates say that over the years Arafat has escaped many ambushes and survived more than a dozen assassination attempts, and his success at Karameh is cited as one of the first manifestations of his baraka.

Arafat is also renowned for his craftiness and his gift for turning crisis into triumph. Karameh was the first well-publicized instance of this ability, but Arafat and the Palestinians have demonstrated their resilience and genius for survival time and again in the years following the battle.

Most important for his own future and that of the Palestinians, Arafat and his followers demonstrated at Karameh the courage and willingness to die for their beliefs. Over the years it often seemed as if much of the world, and particularly Israel and its allies, wished the Palestinians would simply disappear. It seemed obvious, especially to the West, that the nation of Israel was there to stay. But the intractability of the Palestinians, their refusal to relinquish their claim to a homeland, and their willingness to die for that cause proved that the Arabs were in no way less devoted to their land than were the Israelis. It had been argued at the time of Israel's creation that Palestine was sparsely settled, with few Arabs living there, and that those Arab inhabitants were nomads, tenuously connected to the land, while the Jews who came to Palestine were farmers and settlers who built towns and cities and irrigated and improved the land. But by 1948 there were 1.3 million Arabs in Palestine, most of whom were not nomads but town and village dwellers, many educated, with a passionate attachment to their land — an attachment that the battle of Karameh would demonstrate dramatically to the world in 1968.

The battle of Karameh was small in terms of the size of the forces involved and it did not decide a war or topple a dynasty, but it had a significant effect on the morale of the Arabs. Before the battle, Arafat told his fedayeen: "We must shatter the myth of the invincible army." After their defeats in the wars of 1948, 1956, and 1967, many Arabs believed the IDF could not be defeated. By holding his own against the Israelis at Karameh, Arafat shattered that myth and showed that it was possible for a small, poorly equipped but determined force of Palestinians to inflict serious damage on the largest army in the Middle East. Arafat believed that Jordan's contribution to Fatah's success was a good example of what could be accomplished if the Arab nations supported the Palestinians against Israel.

Arafat's strong showing at Karameh gave the Arabs and the Palestinians something of which to be proud. It boosted Palestinian confidence and kept the Arabs interested in Fatah's struggle against Israel. After another Israeli raid on Palestinian guerrilla bases in Jordan, Hussein said, "We are all fedayeen now." After Karameh there was a surge of volunteers wishing to join the ranks of the fedayeen. Abu Jihad, Arafat's second-in-command, spent the four days after the battle in the village of Salt, enrolling recruits for Fatah. In the first 4 days he enlisted nearly 5,000 new soldiers. Twenty-five thousand more fighters signed up in the following 18 months.

Suddenly Israel, viewed only a few months earlier as the David to Arab Goliath, became itself the Goliath, while the hapless Palestinians assumed the role of David.
—THOMAS KIERNAN
American writer, on the effect of the battle at Karameh

The battle of Karameh increased Fatah's prestige as well as its membership and may have saved the group from extinction. In the years before the battle, Fatah's influence in the Arab world was slight, and it had lost many members to rival groups. Within the organization, Arafat faced challenges to his leadership. Some Palestinians thought that Arafat was too militant in his insistence on armed struggle, and others felt he was too cautious.

After Karameh, Arafat was a popular hero. Palestinians both within and outside Fatah cheered him as the only Arab leader to strike a blow against the Israelis. For a time his leadership of Fatah was secure, and the recognition he won as the hero of

Yasir Arafat and aides field questions at a press conference in 1969, the year Fatah and Arafat took control of the PLO. Fatah's insistence that Palestinians act to regain their homeland and its willingness to take guerrilla action against Israel won the organization widespread support.

Karameh helped make Fatah the single most important Palestinian organization.

In 1969 Arafat was elected chairman of the executive committee of the Palestine Liberation Organization (PLO), which was formed in 1964 to represent the displaced Palestinians. The PLO is made up of political organizations, guerrilla groups, labor unions, and professional, women's, and students' organizations. All are represented on the Palestine national council. The PLO charter states that "Palestine is the homeland of the Arab Palestinian people" and that the Palestinians possess the legal right to that homeland. Because the PLO leadership recognized that an entire new generation of children

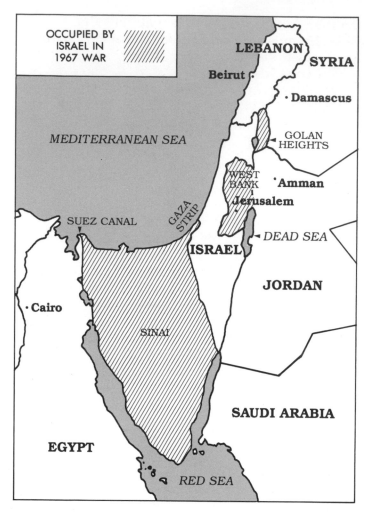

OCCUPIED BY
ISRAEL IN
1967 WAR

LEBANON

SYRIA

Beirut

· Damascus

MEDITERRANEAN SEA

GOLAN
HEIGHTS

WEST
BANK

· Amman

Jerusalem

GAZA STRIP

SUEZ CANAL

ISRAEL

◄ DEAD SEA

JORDAN

· Cairo

SINAI

SAUDI ARABIA

EGYPT

RED SEA

The Middle East. Israel and the occupied territories (the West Bank, Golan Heights, and Gaza Strip) constitute the former region of Palestine.

had been born outside Palestine, with no direct knowledge of the events that led to the creation of Israel and the displacement of the Arabs, the charter emphasizes education. "The Palestinian identity is a genuine, essential, and inherent characteristic . . . transmitted from parents to children," the charter states. That Palestinian identity was not affected by displacement or "the disasters that befell [the Palestinians]"; for the Palestinians it is a "national duty to bring up individual Palestinians in an Arab revolutionary manner. All means of information and education must be adopted in order to acquaint the Palestinian with his country in the most profound manner, both spiritual and material, that is possible. He must be prepared for the armed struggle and ready to sacrifice his wealth and his life in order to win back his homeland and bring about its liberation." The charter goes on to assert that "armed struggle is the only way to liberate Palestine" and that "commando action constitutes the nucleus of the Palestinian popular liberation war."

Fatah became the single largest group within the PLO, primarily because, as Arafat stated in an August 1969 newspaper interview, it was the "first movement that translated the Palestinian aspirations into actions and that by its nature represents the true Palestinian determination." In the years since, the PLO has adopted many of the trappings of a government. It administers hospitals and schools in the camps and has departments of education, public health, intelligence, social services, economy, finance, information, internal security, and defense. More than 100 nations have extended diplomatic recognition to the PLO, and the organization has representatives and ambassadors in many of the world's capitals and major cities. In 1974 the Arab League (an organization of Arab states) declared the PLO the "sole legitimate representative" of the Palestinian people, and in 1976 the PLO became a full-fledged member of the league. Arafat has remained the PLO's chairman, but his hold on power has often been tenuous. He has been decried in Israel and the West as a dangerous fanatic and a terrorist. But among the ranks of the PLO Fatah is regarded as a moderate group, and Arafat has been criticized by more strident elements for softening his approach and becoming too conciliatory toward Israel. The Palestinians have suffered further military setbacks and displacement and exile since Karameh. Like the Palestinian people, Arafat has demonstrated a remarkable resiliency and capacity to adapt. More than any other single individual, he has been responsible for demonstrating that no lasting peace can be possible in the Middle East without addressing the concerns of the Palestinian people.

2

The Problem of Palestine

Like most Arabs, Arafat believes that the Palestinians were unfairly dispossessed of their land by Israel in 1948. The present-day struggle between the Arabs and the Israelis started well before that time, and it has its roots in the long and complicated history of the land that was once called Palestine.

Palestine generally refers to that part of the Middle East bounded by the Mediterranean Sea on the west, the Jordan River on the east, the Sinai Peninsula (now part of Egypt) on the south, and the country of Lebanon on the north. The region got its name from the Philistines, a seafaring people who settled on the Mediterranean coast near the city of Gaza in the 12th century B.C. At different times in its history Palestine has also been called Canaan, Israel, Judah, and Judaea.

Palestine is one of the world's oldest settled regions. It is dry and arid, with fertile patches in the coastal plain and around the Dead Sea and the Sea of Galilee. Throughout much of its history it has been a land of herdsmen, orchard growers, villages, and farms. The 20th century has brought modern highways and urban development, but many people still follow the traditional ways of life.

The Arabs have to learn that Israel is here to stay . . . that even if they did amass enough power to destroy Israel, the United States would never allow it.
—ARNOLD TOYNBEE
British historian

Workers from the United Nations Relief and Works Agency for Palestine Refugees in the Near East (UNRWA) distribute food at a Palestinian camp. The UNRWA also provided health care and educational services, but the poverty and harshness of life made the camps breeding grounds of Palestinian nationalism.

The recorded history of Palestine begins around 1800 B.C., when it was known as Canaan and inhabited by nomadic herdsmen and town-dwelling farmers and traders. Between 1700 and 1100 B.C. many clans of a people called the Hebrews migrated into Canaan from the east and settled there.

The Hebrews were the ancestors of today's Jews. They differed from the other peoples of the early Mediterranean world because they practiced *monotheism* (the worship of one god). Because the Hebrews believed that God had led them into Canaan and given it to them for their homeland, they called it the Promised Land. Many of the stories found in the Old Testament of the Bible are based on events that occurred while the Hebrew tribes were settling in Canaan.

One especially large and powerful group of Hebrews was called the Israelites. To escape a famine, the Israelites migrated to Egypt and lived there for several centuries. In the 13th century B.C. they returned to Canaan under a leader named Moses. Together with the other Hebrew peoples, the Israelites

The prophet Moses looks down at the Promised Land. Jews believe that in the 13th century B.C. Moses led the Israelites—the ancestors of the Jews—out of exile in Egypt into Palestine. They believed Palestine had been promised them in a covenant with their god, whom they called Yahweh.

defeated the Canaanites and formed a Hebrew kingdom, which they named Israel. The southern part of the kingdom later split away and was called Judah, but Hebrew kings and priests ruled in both kingdoms for many years.

After the middle of the 8th century B.C. the Hebrew kingdoms of Palestine fell to a series of conquerors. Even during long periods of oppression by foreign rulers, the Hebrew faith and culture remained strong in Palestine. In the 1st century B.C. the Romans conquered Palestine. The Hebrews revolted against Roman rule, but in A.D. 70 Roman legions destroyed much of the Hebrew capital of Jerusalem, including the Second Temple, and established strict military control. Under the Romans the region was named Palestine and the Hebrews began to be called Jews.

In 132 the Roman emperor Hadrian decided to build a new Roman city on the site of old Jerusalem. Angered, the Jews united in a fierce rebellion. The Romans put down the revolt with great force, destroying nearly 1,000 villages throughout Palestine and killing more than 500,000 people. Most of the surviving Jews fled to North Africa, Spain, and other areas in what would be called the *Diaspora*, a 2,000-year exile from their homeland. A few remained in Palestine, mostly in the northern region called Galilee, but Jewish power in the area had come to an end.

New settlers flowed into Roman Palestine from the lands that are now called Lebanon, Syria, Jordan, and Saudi Arabia. When the Roman Empire split into eastern and western parts at the end of the 4th century, Palestine became part of the Eastern Roman, or Byzantine, Empire, which had its capital at Constantinople, in present-day Turkey. In the 4th century the Byzantine leaders converted to Christianity, the second great monotheistic religion born in the Middle East. They allowed Christians from all parts of the empire to come to Palestine to visit and worship at the places where Jesus Christ had lived, taught, and died. After centuries as the home of the Jewish faith, Palestine became the Christian holy land as well.

From the time of the Crusades in the twelfth and thirteenth centuries until the penetration of England and France in the nineteenth, the Arab region had been a backwater on the global scene.
—THOMAS KIERNAN
American writer

The prophet Muhammad, who founded the religion of Islam in the early 7th century. Much of Islam's ritual and doctrine derived from Judaic and Christian traditions. Like Judaism and Christianity, Islam regards Palestine, particularly the city of Jerusalem, as sacred.

In the early 7th century, at Mecca, on the Arabian Peninsula (in what is now Saudi Arabia), the prophet Muhammad proclaimed the tenets of a new religion. The faith was called Islam, meaning "submission to Allah," which is what its followers, known as Muslims, call God. Allah's revelations to Muhammad are recorded in the *Koran*, the sacred book of Islam. Muslims believe that Muhammad was God's last and truest prophet and that he also revealed himself to, among others, Abraham, the patriarch of the Jews; Moses; and Jesus Christ, whom the Muslims revere as a prophet but do not believe to be the son of God. These others also taught Islam, Muslims believe, but through the ages their teachings have been corrupted or misinterpreted by their followers.

Muhammad urged the tribespeople of Arabia to unite in recognition of Allah. Upon his death in 632, his role as leader of the Muslims fell to the caliph (Arabic for "successor") Abu Bakr. Known as the Conquering Sword of Allah, Abu Bakr called for a *jihad* (holy war) against the neighboring empires. Within a few years, through a combination of conquest and conversion, the Arabs had spread Islam throughout the Middle East, North Africa, and northern India. Today the overwhelming majority of the world's Arabs are Muslims.

Abu Bakr sent 10,000 troops into the land the Arabs called Filastin (Palestine). His successor, the caliph Omar, completed the Islamic conquest of Palestine in 641. Omar built a mosque (an Islamic house of worship) on the site where the great Jewish temple of Jerusalem had stood. Now called the Dome of the Rock, the mosque was erected on the spot where Muslims believe Muhammad ascended into heaven. Already a holy city to Jews and Christians, Jerusalem was soon considered one of the sacred cities of Islam.

Palestine remained part of the Islamic Arab empire for many centuries. Over the years, Arabs became the majority in Palestine, and Islam became its dominant religion. Arab rule in Palestine was not untroubled, however. Between 1095 and 1291 the Christian nations of western Europe launched

A page from a 13th-century Koran, the holy text of Islam. Muslims believe that the Koran is the divine revelation of Allah to his prophet Muhammad. Like most Muslim children, Yasir Arafat learned to read and write by copying out and reciting verses from the Koran.

their own holy war — the Crusades — in an attempt to liberate Palestine from Arab control.

Although the soldiers of the First Crusade succeeded in capturing part of the Holy Land and establishing the Christian kingdom of Jerusalem (accompanied by the massacre of the Muslims and Jews of that city), the Crusades failed. The Arab warrior Saladin recaptured Jerusalem in the 12th century, and the last crusaders were driven out of Palestine by the end of the 13th century.

By the 1500s the Ottoman Empire had begun to establish itself in North Africa, the Middle East, and southeastern Europe. Palestine fell to the Ottomans by 1516 and remained under nominal Ottoman control for the next four centuries. After the rule of Sultan Suleyman the Magnificent from 1520 to 1566, the Ottoman Empire entered a long period of decline, brought on by internal corruption, financial mismanagement, weak rulers, and succession quarrels. Palestine's population dwindled, and its inhabitants had little contact with the rest of the world.

The Dome of the Rock mosque in Jerusalem stands on the former site of the great Jewish temples of Solomon and Herod. Muslims believe that Muhammad made his miraculous nocturnal journey to heaven from this spot. Jews believe that the rock enclosed within the mosque's walls was the site of an altar.

Toward the middle of the 19th century Western nations became interested in the Middle East. Great Britain, France, Germany, and others set up embassies and trading centers in Jerusalem and Gaza. The Ottoman Empire, already dependent upon the European nations for loans and capital, was too weak to keep them out. At the same time, Palestine became the focus of renewed interest on the part of Europe's Jewish population.

The impetus for the restored interest of European Jewry in the Middle East was the mounting influence of Zionism, which advocated the formation of a Jewish homeland, preferably in Palestine. Zionism had existed in various forms for some time, but it gained momentum in the late 19th century after new outbreaks of virulent anti-Semitism in Europe, particularly the pogroms (organized massacres of Jews) in Russia following the assassination of Tsar Alexander II in 1881 and the Dreyfus Affair, in which a Jewish French army officer was falsely accused of passing information to the Germans. The Zionist credo was eloquently articulated by Leon Pinsker and Theodor Herzl, who both argued that anti-Semitism was a permanent fixture in societies where Jews were in the minority and that the only solution was for the Jews to form their own autonomous state.

In 1882 a group of Russian Zionists established the first modern Jewish settlement in Palestine. They cleared land, built homes and farms, and invited other Jews to join them. An early Zionist motto was "a people without a land for a land without a people," but that was not exactly the case. Though sparsely populated, Palestine was home to nearly half a million Arabs with their own hopes and aspirations. The Ottoman Empire was suspicious about the newcomers and attempted to obstruct further settlements but acted cautiously for fear of antagonizing the powerful European nations.

The Zionist movement gained strength. Jews from France, Germany, and especially eastern Europe and Russia settled in Palestine. The World Zionist Organization provided funds for the settlers to buy land. By 1914 Palestine had about 690,000 inhabitants. Of these, 535,000 were Arab Muslims, 85,000 were Jews, and 70,000 were Arab Christians.

Jews pray around 1900 at Jerusalem's Wailing, or Western, Wall, the last surviving remnant of the retaining structure of the Second Temple, whose construction was begun by Herod the Great in 20 B.C. Before the establishment of Israel in 1948, the Western Wall was often the scene of altercations between Arabs and Jews.

An Arab shepherd with his flock in an olive grove in Palestine. The Zionist slogan "a land without people for a people without a land" ignored the fact that Palestine had a sizable Arab population with no desire for a Jewish state in their homeland.

World War I, which began in 1914, rearranged the balance of power in the Middle East. The Ottoman Empire sided with Germany and Austria-Hungary (together they were known as the Central Powers) against Great Britain, France, Russia, and later the United States (the Allies). When the fighting spread to the Middle East, Britain sought to enlist the aid of the Arabs to help fight the Turks. The Arabs realized that rendering assistance to Britain could help them gain their independence from the Ottoman Empire. To gain the support of the Arabs, a British statesman named Sir Henry McMahon wrote to Husan Ibn Ali, an Arab leader, promising British recognition and support for an independent Arab state. Many Arabs then joined the British forces and helped bring about several Allied victories in the Middle East.

The war also made it necessary for Great Britain to court favorable Jewish opinion in Europe and the United States, where more than 3 million European Jews had emigrated after 1880. Most of these émigré Jews were Russian, and the Allies feared they would support the Central Powers because of their hatred of the Russian government, which had encouraged the pogroms. In England influential Zionists such as the chemist Chaim Weizmann and the wealthy financier Lionel Rothschild lobbied the government of Prime Minister David Lloyd George and won the support of several cabinet ministers. In 1917 British foreign secretary Arthur Balfour wrote Rothschild that "His Majesty's Government views with favor the establishment in Palestine of a national home for the Jewish people, and will use their best endeavors to facilitate the achievement of this object, it being clearly understood that nothing shall be done which may prejudice the civil and religious rights of the existing non-Jewish communities in Palestine."

Zionists interpreted the 118-word Balfour Declaration as a pledge of British support for their aims, but its wording was frustratingly ambiguous. The declaration did not assert British support for an autonomous state but for a "national home" and stressed that the rights of the Arabs already there were not to be compromised. There was no discussion of the form this home was to take, its exact geographical location and dimensions, or whether it was to exist within or independent of an Arab state. Likewise, the McMahon letter was unclear as to the extent of the land promised the Arabs and did not attempt to define boundaries. Although the McMahon letter did not mention Palestine at all, the Arabs interpreted it as including that region, where the Jews believed they had been promised an autonomous state in the Balfour Declaration.

In 1917 British and French troops drove German and Ottoman forces from Palestine. At war's end the victorious Allies began the work of distributing the vanquished nations' colonies. Germany's African possessions were parceled out, and the Ottoman Empire was dismembered. After lengthy negotiations, Britain's promise to the Arabs was disregarded. The British and French received mandates from the newly formed League of Nations, an inter-

David Ben-Gurion (center, with white hair) and other Jewish leaders address a gathering of Jews after the United Nations plan to partition Palestine into separate Jewish and Arab states was announced in 1947. Palestine's Arabs rejected the plan and were joined in war against the new state of Israel by troops from the neighboring Arab states.

national peacekeeping organization, to administer the Arab areas and prepare them for self-government. France received the mandate for what would become Syria and Lebanon; Britain received the mandate for Palestine and the future states of Iraq and Jordan.

Britain's mandate over Palestine affirmed the Balfour Declaration and, echoing the language found there, asserted that Britain should be responsible for establishing a Jewish national home. A Jewish agency was to be established to advise the British administration in Palestine, and Jewish immigration and "close settlement . . . on the land" was to be encouraged, although the rights of "other sections of the population" (the Arabs) were to be protected. English, Hebrew, and Arabic were established as Palestine's official languages. Under the British, Zionists came to Palestine in increased numbers. The Arabs felt betrayed. Instead of the independence they believed they had been pledged, the Arabs were now governed by a British admin-

Palestinian refugees at a camp in Jordan await the distribution of milk and other food. By the late 1960s a generation of Palestinians had grown up in the camps. Often poor and unemployed, they made willing recruits for Fatah and other guerrilla groups.

משטרת ישראל
אין מעבר!
גבול לפניך
STOP!-BORDER
IN FRONT OF YOU
ATTENTION!
FRONTIERE

אסור להוציא
לשבור או להחזיק
אלמוגים
בכל שטח הים והחוף

מועצה מקומית אילת

istration working hand in hand with Zionist organizations to establish a Jewish state. Hostility
between the Arabs and the Zionist newcomers escalated into violence.

Angered by the rapid growth of the Jewish population, Palestinian Arabs rioted for 3 days in 1920,
resulting in the death of 135 Jews. In another riot
a year later, 47 Jews were killed, after which the
British police killed 48 Arabs. The Jewish settlers
continued to come, tension mounted, and violent
confrontations continued. Both sides accused the
British of favoring the other. The long tragedy of
Arab-Jewish relations in the Middle East had begun. Each side claimed the sanction of history and
religion; neither was able to recognize the legitimate
aspirations of the other; political compromises were
rejected. In the words of Edward Said, a well-known
Palestinian professor of literature, each had chosen
the other "for a struggle whose roots seem to go
deeper . . . and whose future seems less thinkable
and resolvable each year."

**Signs in the Sinai Peninsula
mark the Israeli-Egyptian
border. From 1948 until
1988, the Palestinians refused to recognize Israel's
right to exist. During that
same period Israel rejected all
proposals to hold talks with
the PLO and continued to do
so after the PLO officially recognized Israel in November
1988.**

3

A Lifetime of Resistance

Yasir Arafat was born Rahman Abdul Rauf Arafat al-Qudwa al-Husseini on August 24, 1929. (Arafat, in Yasir's case a given, not a family, name, is the name of the mountain near Mecca where Muslims believe Muhammad was made God's messenger. Arafat's family names are al-Qudwa — his father's — and al-Husseini — his mother's. Yasir is a nickname given him later.) Arafat and the PLO are very secretive about many of the details of his life. He claims that he was born in Jerusalem in a house only a short distance from the Dome of the Rock that was bulldozed once the Israelis took control of the West Bank and all of Jerusalem in 1967. By stating that he was born in Jerusalem Arafat wishes to emphasize that he is a Palestinian by birth, but it is more likely that he was actually born in Cairo, Egypt's largest city.

Kinship and family relationships are of great importance in the Arab world, and Arafat was born into a family of wealth and impeccable bloodlines. His mother, Hamida Khalifa al-Husseini, traced her ancestry on her father's side to Fatima, daughter of Muhammad, and therefore to Muhammad himself, which afforded her great prestige. She was also re-

An Arab tea vendor in East Jerusalem, sometimes referred to as the Old City, in the 1940s. East Jerusalem is home to the most sacred sites of Judaism, Islam, and Christianity. The Old City remained under Arab control following the partition of Palestine but was captured by the Israelis during the Six-Day War.

lated to Abdul Khader al-Husseini, one of the leading fighters against the British and the Jews during the years of the British mandate, and Haj Amin al-Husseini, a violent anti-Zionist who was appointed grand mufti of Jerusalem — a ceremonial position somewhat equivalent to mayor — by the British in 1921.

Arafat's father, Abdul Rauf al-Qudwa, was descended from a family of wealthy merchants and landowners in the Gaza area. His primary business was concerned with foodstuffs, and he was known as the founder of a factory for making cheese that was sold throughout the Arab world.

Arafat grew up in a climate of fierce Arab nationalism. Hostility between the Arabs and the Jews grew during the 1920s as the number of new settlers coming to Palestine increased. Attacks on Jewish settlers and property became common. Among the most unyielding anti-Zionist Arab leaders was Arafat's relative Amin al-Husseini. As Arab militance increased, violence was also directed at those within the Arab community believed to have cooperated with the Jews or British. Particularly suspect were merchants who did business with the Jews or the British and landowners who sold land to Jewish settlers. Arafat's father had once owned a business that sold religious articles to Jews and still managed commercial interests in Jerusalem, Jaffa, and Gaza. He was accused of profiting from the Zionist settlement of Palestine and was the target of reprisals. In 1927 he was beaten, family members and business partners were threatened, and his house in Gaza was bombed, which led him to move his family to Cairo.

On the day before Arafat was born, violent rioting broke out in the streets of Jerusalem. The immediate cause was the attempt by Jews to pray at the Wailing, or Western, Wall, which is a portion of the wall surrounding the Dome of the Rock mosque and is revered by the Jews as the sole surviving remnant of the great temple that was destroyed by the Romans. Arab sensitivity to the possible desecration of their holy place had been heightened by a campaign to repair and restore the mosque spearheaded

Rahman, as Arafat was called by his family, passed the first few years of his life as most Arab children do—generally ignored by his father and totally within his mother's embrace.

—THOMAS KIERNAN
American writer

by Amin al-Husseini and the Supreme Muslim Council, the main Arab political organ in Jerusalem. Arabs set upon the Jewish worshipers, and the fighting soon spread throughout the city. Hundreds of Arabs and Jews were killed.

Arafat has said that his childhood was an unhappy time. He was the sixth of seven children. The oldest was his sister Inam. His two other sisters were named Yosra and Khadiga, and two older brothers were named Gamal and Moustapha. The youngest child was Arafat's brother Fathe. Family members and friends remember Rahman, as Arafat was known as a child, as an abnormally quiet, withdrawn child. His sister Inam once told a reporter that he was called Yasir from an early age because it is an Arabic word that means "easygoing" or "no problem." He was noted for the steady, penetrating gaze of his protruding eyes; he usually was able to stare down other children who insulted him or tried to start fights.

When Yasir was four his mother died of a kidney disease, and he and Fathe were sent to Jerusalem to live with relatives. Four years later Abdul Rauf married again, and Yasir and Fathe returned to the family home in Cairo. The new stepmother did not

Haj Amin al-Husseini (in white turban) meets with British officials and local Palestinian representatives in 1929. A relative of Arafat's, al-Husseini was the religious head of the Muslim community in Jerusalem and an important Palestinian nationalist leader.

get along with the Arafat children, who said she was cruel. Their house was filled with screaming and fighting. After only a few months, in response to his children's complaints, Arafat's father divorced his second wife. He married for a third time soon after, but this time he took precautions to maintain order in his household. The new wife was given separate quarters, and Inam was given the responsibility of raising her younger brothers and sisters. Although he remained fond of Inam, the young Arafat often argued with her. He was a very independent child and considered himself his own boss from about the age of 10.

Like all Muslim boys, Arafat and his brothers received a great deal of religious schooling. Their tutor in the Koran was their mother's uncle Yusuf Awad al-Akbar. Arafat was an overweight, awkward, and effeminate child who was the butt of much teasing by his schoolmates. His brothers underwent their religious lessons with a degree of reluctance, but under his great-uncle's tutelage young Arafat revealed a mental agility and prodigious gift of recall. Yusuf was quick to praise his new star pupil, whom he was convinced possessed great talents, and Arafat soon became devoted to his teacher. He volunteered for extra lessons and spent most of his free hours listening to the older man speak on the tenets of Islam and his family's history. Yusuf Awad believed that the al-Husseini family was special by virtue of its descent from the prophet Muhammad, and he was convinced that young Arafat had been sent as a gift to restore the greatness of the family name. He had no love for the boy's father, Abdul Rauf, and he denigrated the father to the son, emphasizing that the al-Qudwas were nothing more than shopkeepers and merchants. Because Abdul Rauf was a somewhat cold and distant man, young Arafat found it easy to accept criticism of him, and he gave his love and loyalty to his great-uncle instead.

At about this same time, in 1936, Haj Amin al-Husseini organized a general strike by Arabs in Jerusalem. The Arabs also formed guerrilla groups for attacks against Jewish and British targets. The strike lasted six months and turned into a wide-

British troops patrol the town of Acre (Akko) toward the
end of the Arab revolt of 1936. Aggravated by increased
Jewish immigration from Europe, tension between Arabs
and Jews in Palestine had erupted into six months of fighting between the two groups.

spread Arab revolt, which required considerable British military effort to suppress. The British forced al-Husseini's removal as head of the Muslim Council, and he fled to Germany.

Arafat's father was radicalized by the events in Palestine. His business interests often took him to Jerusalem, and he returned angered by what he saw there. He told his children impassioned tales of how the Jews were robbing the Arabs of their homeland. Abdul Rauf's newfound political commitment moved him to join the Muslim Brotherhood, a secret organization founded by Hassan al-Banna in 1928. The Muslim Brotherhood's Islamic fundamentalism had profound political connotations. It advocated an independent Egypt with a constitution based on the Koran and Islamic law. Egypt had been ruled by Great Britain since the late 1800s, and the Muslim Brotherhood saw the British presence as a danger-ous secular influence that was weakening the na-tion. It rejected all contact with Western nations and formed guerrilla groups to fight the British and those Egyptian politicians it believed were cooper-

A British soldier aims his ma-chine gun from a rooftop in East Jerusalem in 1938 fol-lowing a week-long siege of the Arab quarter of the Old City by British troops. One year later, with World War II imminent, Britain's desire to placate the Arabs led the country to renounce its com-mitment to the establish-ment of a Jewish state.

ating in maintaining British rule, likening its struggle to the traditional Islamic concept of the jihad, or holy war against the infidels (unbelievers). Al-Banna's group was also concerned with Palestine, where its Arab and Muslim brothers were also under Britain's thumb, with an added danger presented by the ongoing flow of Jewish immigration. The Brotherhood found adherents among the many Palestinian Arabs living in Egypt. Arafat's father became well known in the community as an organizer for the group, and he was often seen carrying an old British rifle as a symbol of the Brotherhood's and his own militancy.

Meanwhile, the intrafamilial war continued to rage. Arafat had begun to display his disdain for his father through flagrant acts of disobedience, and Abdul Rauf was angry with Yusuf Awad for turning his son against him. Yusuf Awad offered to buy Arafat from his father (a not unheard of practice in the Arab world), but Abdul Rauf refused. Yusuf then continued his efforts to win the boy's heart and mind and told Arafat that his father had profited by his business dealings with the Jews. Abdul Rauf was irate when he discovered that Yusuf was spreading the old allegations. In the summer of 1939 Yusuf Awad was found garroted and hanged, the trademark method of assassination of the Muslim Brotherhood.

The death of his great-uncle shocked and saddened Yasir. Not long after, his father moved the family back to the city of Gaza, perhaps to avoid police questioning about Yusuf Awad's murder. Some sources suggest that Abdul Rauf was ordered to move to Gaza by Hassan al-Banna himself, who was eager for the Muslim Brotherhood to establish itself in Palestine. In Gaza, Abdul Rauf made contact with Palestinians active in the fight to liberate their country, most of whom were loyal to his kinsman Haj Amin al-Husseini.

Arafat resumed his schooling and came under the influence of Majid Halaby, a young teacher, born in southern Lebanon and educated in Paris, who was active in the resistance movement. Once again Arafat was considered odd and either teased or ignored by his classmates, but Halaby was struck by his obvious intelligence and physical resemblance to Yasir al-Birah, the slain leader of a guerrilla group to which Halaby belonged. Some biographers claim that it was Halaby who first dubbed Arafat "Yasir."

Abdul Rauf's attempts to unite the Arab resistance groups failed, and the movement in Gaza remained split between those loyal to the Muslim Brotherhood and the followers of Haj Amin al-Husseini and his nephew Abdul Khader, who was acting as leader while Amin was in exile. Abdul Rauf was able to convince Halaby to join the Muslim Brotherhood. Fearing retribution by Amin's forces, Halaby gave up his teaching post and went into hiding at a house provided by Abdul Rauf, who also paid him a stipend to train several of his young students, including Arafat, as guerrilla fighters.

The year 1939 proved to be crucial in the history of Palestine. In September Germany's Nazi dictator, Adolf Hitler, invaded Poland, beginning World War II. By that point he had begun to lay the groundwork for his "final solution," which in its ultimate form aimed at nothing less than the annihilation of Europe's entire Jewish population, estimated at between 8 and 10 million. By war's end in 1945 more than 6 million Jews had perished at the hands of the Nazis and their collaborators. In some nations the entire Jewish population was virtually eradicated. Ninety percent of the Jews in Poland, Czechoslovakia, and Greece were killed; 80 percent of the Jews in Holland lost their lives. Much of the Jewish cultural life in Europe was destroyed forever.

With Hitler's onslaught, Jewish immigration to Palestine took on a new, desperate character. The Nazi genocide made immigration a matter of personal, national, and cultural survival. Between 1917 and 1939 the Jewish population in Palestine increased from 85,000 to more than 500,000, but the Jews still numbered fewer than the Arabs. The sheer volume of new immigrants and the corresponding rise in tension between the Arabs and Jews made the Palestinian mandate increasingly burdensome for Britain to administer. Now at war with Germany, the British wished to garner support among the Arabs, who might prove useful in the war effort. In 1939 the British government issued a white paper (official government report) that announced it would no longer feel bound by the Balfour Declaration, whose "ambiguity" was a "fundamental cause of unrest and hostility between Arabs and Jews." The White Paper asserted that the Balfour Declaration did not mean that "Palestine should be converted into a Jewish State against the will of the Arab population of the country." Accordingly, Britain's new aim was to allow Palestine to develop as an independent country in which the interests of both the Arabs and Jews were represented. The White Paper acknowledged as legitimate the Arab concern that continued Jewish immigration would soon make the Arabs a minority in their own country but recognized that events in Europe made Jewish immigration of special importance. Jewish immigration was fixed at 15,000 per year for the next 5 years and was then to occur only with Arab concurrence; restrictions on land ownership were also fixed.

Neither the Arabs nor the Jews were pleased with the White Paper. The Zionists interpreted it as a betrayal of what the British had promised them. The restrictions on immigration were unacceptable, particularly as it was now a matter of life and death for many European Jews. While the mainstream Jewish Agency and Labor Zionists led by David Ben-Gurion believed that defeating Nazi Germany was of the first priority and sought to cooperate with Britain in order to aid the war effort, militant Jewish groups such as the *Lehi* and the *Irgun* carried out guerrilla warfare against the British. The Irgun's most famous operation was the demolition of the King David Hotel in Jerusalem in 1946.

Having been victimized previously by British promises, the Arabs were wary of further assurances. Haj Amin and the Arab leadership rejected the White Paper. As the British had feared, Arab resistance groups — both those of the Muslim Brotherhood and those loyal to Amin al-Husseini — made overtures to Germany for arms and assistance, although Abdul Khader al-Husseini and many of the

> *Of all the ideas that the Middle East has imported from the West, none has been more popular than nationalism.*
> —ARTHUR GOLDSCHMIDT, JR.
> American historian

The barbed wire strewn between Jewish and Arab sections of Jerusalem in the spring of 1948 testifies to the tension in the city on the eve of the British departure. With the withdrawal of the British administration and military, Israel declared its independence, and full-scale warfare began.

younger resistance leaders did not wish the movement to associate itself with the Nazi regime. They argued that it should be emphasized that the Arab quarrel with the Jews was rooted in a political question — control over the land of Palestine — and was not based on racial hatred, as were the noxious policies and practices of the Nazis. However, in Germany in 1942 Haj Amin lobbied the Nazis for Arab independence. He publicly endorsed the Nazis' policies regarding the Jews and made radio broadcasts to North Africa and the Middle East in which he urged the Arabs to assist the German forces when they arrived. (At the time Nazi forces were moving east across North Africa.)

A rift between Halaby and Abdul Rauf soon developed, with Halaby urging violent action, in accordance with Haj Amin's radio broadcasts, and Abdul Rauf counseling patience and organizational work, as ordered by Hassan al-Banna. Halaby left Abdul's home, and Arafat, devoted to Halaby, went with him, becoming his chief assistant. Arab hopes for a German liberation died with the Nazis' defeat at the Battle of El Alamein in Egypt in November

1942. Halaby, who now took the *nom de guerre* (literally, war name) Abu Khalid, spent most of his time training his young charges, and the rivalry between him and Abdul Rauf's group intensified. When Halaby brought his group to Jerusalem to reunite with Abdul Khader al-Husseini, Abdul Rauf and his supporters, many of whom had sons in Halaby's group, objected and had Halaby killed. Arafat and his other followers were told Halaby had met his death in a guerrilla action.

Although only 15, Arafat was directed by Abdul Khader to work to unite his father's Muslim Brotherhood organization with Abdul Khader and Haj Amin's group, now known as the Palestine Arab party. A reconciliation between the two factions, and between father and son, was achieved. Arafat vowed to carry on Halaby's work of freeing Palestine and pledged his loyalty to Abdul Khader, unaware that he had been involved in Halaby's murder. Abdul Khader convinced Arafat that he could best serve the movement by returning to school in Gaza and recruiting future soldiers from among his classmates. Arafat did as he was instructed and formed

the Martyr Abu Khalid Society; by 1946 it had some
300 members. His schoolmates noticed how the former object of their jokes had grown in self-assurance
and presence.

World War II ended in August 1945 with the Allies
(the United States, Great Britain, France, and the
Soviet Union) victorious over Germany, Italy, and
Japan. With the war over, Israeli resistance to the
British escalated. In 1947 Britain announced its
intention to relinquish the mandate, quit Palestine,
and refer the problem to the United Nations (UN).
Its troops and other personnel would be withdrawn
by August 1948. The UN's solution was to partition
Palestine into two separate states, one Jewish and
one Arab. The Arabs bitterly rejected this proposal,
and in early 1948 full-scale fighting between the
Arabs and Jews began. The Palestinian Arabs were
aided by troops from neighboring Arab nations, but
the Arab war effort was plagued by factionalism and
poor leadership and organization. In contrast, the
Jews had profited by their cooperation with the British military during the war, and the more than
40,000 men of the *Haganah*, the main Jewish defense force, and the Irgun were extremely well
trained and well disciplined, if not particularly well
equipped. When the British completed their withdrawal on May 14, 1948, the Jews immediately proclaimed the establishment of the independent state
of Israel. Egypt, Iraq, Syria, Lebanon, and Transjordan (later Jordan) declared war on the new nation, but the Israelis had the best of the fighting.
When hostilities ceased in January, Israel had expanded its borders beyond those established by the
partition plan, adding to its territory western Galilee, the city of Jaffa, the new city of Jerusalem, and
the corridor between Jerusalem and the coast.

In the early days of the war, before the end of the
mandate, Arafat and his group helped smuggle guns
from Egypt to Jerusalem. He may have been directly
guided in his efforts by Haj Amin, who had returned
to the Middle East and established himself in Cairo,
receiving recognition from the Arab League as the
spokesman for the rights of the Palestinians. Arafat
also said in later years that at this time he received

secret military training from a German officer who came to Palestine with his relatives. After the British withdrawal, Arafat joined the Egyptian army and was given noncombatant duties, such as carrying food and water. He expected the Arab victory to be complete in a few short weeks, but soon the reality of the Arab failure set in. Arafat believed the Palestinians were defeated because their Arab allies were either unwilling or unable to give them sufficient support.

The worst fear of the Palestinian Arabs had come true. The majority of the Arab population of Palestine (estimated at slightly more than one million in 1948), perhaps as many as 700,000 Arabs, was displaced by the Israeli victory. Most have never returned to their homes, villages, and farms. The reasons for the Arab displacement are still disputed by Israelis and Palestinians and remain at the heart of their conflict. Some of the Arabs fled simply to avoid the fighting, but Israelis argue that most of them left their homeland because they did not wish to live in a Jewish state or were ordered to do so by radio broadcasts from the Arab nations, which urged them to abandon their homes and regroup in the Arab countries, where preparations for the final offensive against Israel were taking place. Palestine's Arabs, the Israelis argue, were betrayed by their Arab brethren into surrendering their land or left voluntarily.

Most Palestinians believe differently. They assert that research indicates no such broadcasts occurred. According to the Palestinians the Arabs were forced from their land by the Israeli military and not allowed to return. The truth encompasses both positions. At the small Arab village of Deir Yassin, near Jerusalem, in April 1948, Irgun commandos massacred 254 Arabs, many of them women and children. It has been alleged that the killings were planned to send a message to other Arabs, to frighten them into abandoning their lands. The bodies of the dead were not buried, and prisoners from the village were paraded blindfolded on trucks through Jerusalem. Menachem Begin, the Irgun's commander and later prime minister of Israel, wrote

The [UN] partition plan was certainly not a peaceful resolution to the contest for Palestine. . . . Each [side] committed brutal acts of terrorism against innocent civilians.
—ARTHUR GOLDSCHMIDT, JR.
American writer

that reports of the massacre were Arab propaganda but conceded that they had a positive effect in that they "spread a legend of terror among Arabs and Arab soldiers, who were seized with panic at the mention of Irgun soldiers," leading to further evacuations. Whether Deir Yassin was a calculated outrage intended to terrorize other Arab civilians or a horrifying excess of war, there is no doubt the Israeli military forcibly evicted many Arab civilians. Israeli military records contain many documents detailing such forced evacuations, and in his 1979 memoirs former prime minister Yitzhak Rabin told of how his unit drove 50,000 Arabs from their homes in Lod and Ramle and forced them across the borders. The homes and villages of those who fled were often razed. Arafat asserts that the Arabs were forced from more than 500 towns and villages and that 385 of these were totally destroyed. In later years the houses of those suspected of being Palestinian partisans were blown up. For the displaced Palestinians, the memory of their lost homeland is as crucial

Israeli soldiers inspect an Egyptian fighter plane downed during the fighting in Palestine in 1948. Israel's military forces defeated the Arab armies, and the Israeli nation doubled its size.

to their unification and sense of nation as the image of the Promised Land was to the Jews during their Diaspora. American writer David Shipler puts it another way: "The longing for return is as integral to the Palestinian nationalism that has evolved since 1948 as it was, and is, to the Jewish Zionism that has moved thinkers and activists from the 19th century onward."

At war's end Arafat sought a meeting with Palestinian leaders, still headed by Haj Amin al-Husseini. He asked them for money to pay for weapons and training to carry on the fighting. Husseini was no help, and Arafat returned to Gaza in despair. Someone in his family suggested that he go to the United States to college, as many Palestinians from well-to-do families were doing at the time. He agreed and applied for a visa to enter the United States.

While waiting for his visa, Arafat led a gang of young guerrillas in Gaza. Ostensibly in training to resume the war with Israel, they terrorized any Palestinians who supported King Abdullah of Transjordan's plan to annex the West Bank. Their tactics sometimes included assassination. When his American visa had not arrived by the summer of 1950, Arafat enrolled in a civil engineering course at the University of Cairo, where he resumed his career as a student organizer, this time for the Muslim Brotherhood's struggle in Egypt against the British and King Farouk. By now Arafat had rejected Haj Amin and his supporters, convinced that they were concerned more with factional fighting than opposing Israel, a tendency that culminated in the assassination of King Abdullah at the al-Aqsa mosque in Jerusalem in July 1951. In Arafat's second year at the school a young Egyptian army officer, Gamal Abdel Nasser, led a military coup that overthrew Farouk. Nasser installed Mohammed Naguib as president. Soon afterward, Arafat and some fellow students presented Naguib with a petition urging him not to forget the Palestinian cause. It was signed in blood.

That same year Arafat joined the Palestinian Student Federation (PSF). Although its membership was officially limited to university students, other

King Farouk was a corrupt bungler who did not give a damn about the Palestinian people.
—YASIR ARAFAT

Palestinians were allowed to join. The PSF was dedicated to working against Israel and liberating Palestine. With the help of contacts in the Muslim Brotherhood, Arafat managed to get permission to establish a military training camp on university grounds. For two years he led other Palestinian students in physical training, mock military maneuvers, and other exercises. Arafat's interest in his classes was slight, but he became fascinated with explosives and learned how to make homemade bombs.

Many of Arafat's closest friendships began at this point in his life. Salah Khalaf, who later became a top executive in the PLO, was Arafat's assistant in the PSF. Another friend and adviser was Hamid Abu Sitta, a disciple of Abdul Khader al-Husseini whom Arafat had met a few years earlier. It has also been reported that Arafat was engaged to be married at this time but that the wedding plans were canceled when the woman's father discovered Arafat's true identity and connections with the Muslim Brotherhood. His fiancée says that she became terrified of Arafat when she realized he was responsible for the murder of the father of some Jewish friends of hers. Arafat has denied ever knowing the woman.

In the fall of 1953 some of the PSF's members questioned Arafat's performance as their leader. He was accused of being arrogant and dictatorial and of filling important positions with his compatriots from Gaza, most of whom were not students. Arafat and his supporters were voted out of office. The resourceful Arafat was unfazed; he simply formed a new group, called the General Union of Palestinian Students (GUPS).

The GUPS grew rapidly, in part because one of its members knew someone who owned a printing press. Arafat persuaded the Egyptian authorities to let the GUPS print and distribute a student newsletter called *The Voice of Palestine*. Through this newsletter, which had nothing to do with student affairs, the GUPS made contact with Palestinians throughout the Arab world and encouraged them to form small units, or cells, of underground guerrillas, which would be used to dart across Israel's borders to carry out acts of terrorism and sabotage against Israeli power plants, military patrol vehicles, and roads in order to provoke Israel to strike back against its Arab neighbors. Once this happened, the GUPS believed, the Arab nations would be forced to strike back against Israel in turn. In the ensuing war, part or all of Palestine could be seized from the Jews. Arafat felt that the Arab nations were insufficiently committed to the Palestinian cause and would simply ignore the problem if allowed to do so. The guerrilla raids were one way of ensuring that the Arab nations did not forget the Palestinians.

A young man in Gaza named Khalil Wazir was one of many who read *The Voice of Palestine* regularly. He led a small fedayeen group of his own and was once jailed by the Egyptian authorities for making bombs. In 1954 he and Arafat met and became friends. Later known as Abu Jihad, Wazir was to become Arafat's second-in-command in the PLO.

By 1955 Arafat had decided that he was ready for a wider base of power than the GUPS offered. He wanted to unite all of the Palestinian student groups into a single large organization. The PSF resisted, but after several of its members were killed it agreed to join the GUPS. Arafat was elected chairman.

A year earlier Nasser had ousted Naguib and assumed power himself. An advocate of pan-Arabism — the notion that by virtue of their common language, religion, culture, and heritage the Arabs constituted one nation and should unite to fight Israel and the continued colonial influence of the West, particularly Great Britain and the United States — Nasser supported the Palestinian cause and armed and trained commando units in Gaza for attacks on Israel. Soon after, a troop of Palestinian and Egyptian soldiers was ambushed and killed by the Israelis in Gaza. Hoping to force Nasser to retaliate, Arafat and Wazir staged massive student demonstrations. In Gaza, Wazir led a group of students waving handkerchiefs dipped in blood. They skirmished with the Egyptian authorities and set fire to their offices. In Cairo, Arafat met with Nasser,

A rally was announced at which Yasir would speak to all Palestinian and other interested [college] students. Implicit in the language . . . was the threat that the Palestinian students who failed to attend would regret their failure.
—THOMAS KIERNAN
American writer, on Arafat's attempt to garner the support of Palestinian students

who agreed to let him visit Gaza (which was then a restricted zone under Egyptian military contol) for three days. During that time, Arafat set up new cells of fedayeen and planned guerrilla attacks on Israel. Nasser's support for the Palestinians led Arafat to gradually sever his ties with the Muslim Brotherhood. It was no longer possible to support both. After a member of the Brotherhood attempted to assassinate Nasser in 1954, he had most of the group's members arrested, severely crippling the organization's effectiveness.

Arafat completed his studies and received an engineering degree in July 1956. No longer a student, he had to give up the chairmanship of the GUPS. He formed a new group, the Union of Palestinian Graduates (UPG), and named himself chairman. Under cover of this organization his political and fedayeen activities continued. He also went to work for an Egyptian construction company.

That same month saw the outbreak of the second war between Israel and Egypt, precipitated when Nasser decided to nationalize the Suez Canal, which connects the Mediterranean and Red seas. The canal was built by the French, owned mainly by the British, and relied on as a vital waterway by the Western nations. Britain, France, and Israel all desired to act against Nasser. Israel was tired of his sponsorship of the Palestinians, Britain wished to regain its lost influence in the Middle East and reopen the canal, and France was angered by Nasser's support for freedom fighters in its colony of Algeria. The three nations agreed to attack Egypt together. Arafat volunteered for service in the Egyptian army. He was given the rank of second lieutenant and assigned to a bomb-disposal squad in the city of Port Said.

The Egyptians were beaten decisively on the battlefield. Although the fighting stopped after a few weeks, mainly because of pressure placed on Britain and France by the United States and the UN, and Nasser became an Arab hero for defying the Israelis and standing up to two powerful Western nations, Arafat and other Palestinian rebels were forced to admit that the fighting had not produced the de-

sired results. The Arabs had again lost territory to the Israelis, who now occupied the Sinai Peninsula and the Gaza Strip. Although both were returned to Egypt under the terms of the cease-fire, the largest and most powerful of the Arab nations had been soundly defeated once more, and the Palestinian cause had suffered a severe setback.

Arafat's bomb-disposal skills were highly valued, and after the Suez crisis he was offered a promotion and asked to stay in the Egyptian army. He declined. "I told them I had another job," he said. Tired of relying on the other Arab nations for support, he was now ready to begin organizing a new, larger Palestinian movement.

Palestinians in the Gaza Strip greet Egyptian president Gamal Abdel Nasser in 1956. Nasser became the head of the largest Arab nation in 1952, and his advocacy of pan-Arabism soon made him the most important leader of the Arab world.

4
Fatah and the PLO

Because Arafat was not yet a figure of world importance, newspapers took little notice of his activities during the next few years, and he has not said much about this period of his life. Accounts of his travels in the mid-1950s differ in details. Sometimes he vanished entirely from sight, perhaps to receive guerrilla training in Egypt, Algeria, or other countries sympathetic to the Palestinian cause.

Nevertheless, it is known that his first opportunity to present his nationalist movement to the outside world came in March 1957, when the Soviet Union and other countries of the Communist bloc invited several Arab nations to send representatives to an international convention of students in Prague, Czechoslovakia. Although he was no longer a student or an official member, Arafat led an eight-member delegation representing the GUPS.

Arafat welcomed the opportunity to attend the convention because he hoped to establish a network of Palestinian student organizations throughout Europe, where many Palestinians were living, working, and studying. He also wished to obtain a commitment to supply weapons and money from his Communist hosts.   In Prague, the delegation split

I would say that in the first year, Yasir raised about twenty thousand English pounds. But that is not all he did. He also recruited more people to the committee, including myself.
—OMAR AL-HATAB
member of Fatah, on
Arafat's work for the group

Arafat addresses a summit conference of nonaligned nations in Havana, Cuba, in 1979. In the little more than 20 years since Arafat had begun Fatah, he achieved widespread diplomatic recognition for the Palestine liberation movement.

Arafat responds to questions at a Damascus, Syria, press conference. In the late 1960s Fatah and other guerrilla groups frequently attacked Israel from bases in Jordan, Lebanon, and Syria. The targets were usually those Fatah regarded as the instruments of Israeli government policy directed against the Palestinians.

into two factions, divided over Arafat's attempts to dominate the group. The conference's sponsors were not impressed with the Arafat delegation, and he did not receive the commitments he was seeking. Five of the Palestinians returned to Egypt after the meeting, but Arafat, Khalil Wazir, and Salah Khalaf remained in Czechoslovakia, where they soon received disturbing news from Cairo. The Egyptian secret police had discovered a plot to assassinate Nasser, who had become unpopular with some of the more militant Arab groups because of his suppression of the Muslim Brotherhood. Arafat heard from friends in Cairo that the police suspected him of being involved in the plot, and he decided not to return to Egypt.

Instead, Arafat, Wazir, and Khalaf went to Stuttgart, West Germany. Several of Wazir's cousins were enrolled in the university there, and West Germany had a large population of Palestinian students. The three traveled from Czechoslovakia to West Ger-

many using borrowed passports, with their own photographs pasted over those of University of Stuttgart students.

Although he was able to keep busy in Stuttgart recruiting students for the liberation movement, Arafat grew eager to return to the Middle East. Knowing that he was still liable to arrest in Egypt, he applied for engineering jobs in Saudi Arabia and Kuwait.

Like many of the newly formed nations around the Persian Gulf, Saudi Arabia and Kuwait were suddenly oil rich and were experiencing construction booms. Skilled workers were in demand, and Arafat was offered jobs in both countries. He chose Saudi Arabia — but planned to stop in Cairo and Gaza first.

In Gaza he was angered by what he saw. Most of the Palestinians he visited had been totally demoralized by the most recent Israeli victory. Even those who had been active in the liberation movement, such as his father and brothers, were disheartened. The Israelis were too strong, they told Arafat. It was time to resign themselves to the fact that Israel could not be defeated. Arafat refused to listen. He made a secret visit to Iraq to meet two army officers who were planning to assassinate that country's king Faisal. The Egyptian government was not pleased to hear of the meeting. When Arafat learned that the secret police were looking for him, he knew it was time to leave. He had hoped to go to Saudi Arabia, which was becoming the most powerful of the Arab oil kingdoms, but had not yet received the necessary visa, so he made his way to Kuwait instead.

Kuwait had been made a British protectorate after the war, which meant that it was under British supervision while preparing itself for independence, which would come in 1961. Arafat realized that he would have to move carefully in order to continue his political activities without attracting the attention of the British. He went to work for the Department of Water Supply and started his own construction company on the side, using Palestinian workers. He quickly demonstrated good business sense and an ability to make money. He could have become a millionaire in Kuwait if he had not been a revolutionary, he once said, but within days of his arrival in that country he had taken the first steps toward a new Palestinian organization.

Arafat sent for Wazir, and the two began to lay their plans. By September 1957 they had agreed that their task was to remind Israel and the other nations of the world that the Palestinian problem still existed. Wazir said, "We knew that guns spoke louder than words in the world of the big powers," but both men recognized the need for planning and organization before they began operations. Their immediate goals were to publish a newsletter or magazine that would attract new members, as *The Voice of Palestine* had done in their student days, and to buy weapons. Both goals required money, and Arafat donated much of his income to the cause. In the early days of the group, Arafat concerned himself primarily with fund-raising and recruiting, and Wazir handled ideology. Thomas Kiernan, an Arafat biographer, quotes one group member as saying: "Yasir was the financial genius in those first years. He made it more or less an official practice to get contributions to the organization from those who came to him seeking construction contracts. It soon became known that to get approval for a contract a company would have to donate a certain percentage of the contract's worth to the Palestine Liberation Committee, which is what we were calling Fatah back there in the beginning." Arafat also began cautiously recruiting fellow Palestinians into the movement and forming cells of three to five members.

The Palestinian movement needed secrecy. Although the Arab governments publicly supported the Palestinian cause and helped provide for the refugees, from Arafat's point of view they had done little to help free Palestine. Jordan even went so far as to annex the West Bank, an act opposed by most Palestinians. Many of the Palestinians were reluctant to assimilate themselves into other Arab societies because they feared that in so doing they would lose their own distinct nationality, and the host governments often resented such independence, par-

ticularly when they were being told that it was their
duty to provide the arms and soldiers that would
free the Palestinian homeland. Some leaders feared
that the activities of Palestinian guerrilla and liberation groups were likely to bring Israeli retaliation
upon the host governments, and they were apt to
view the groups' activities as interference in their
own internal affairs. Many of the Arab governments
were reluctant to provoke further hostility.

Arafat and many of his followers adopted *noms
de guerre.* In choosing their aliases they adopted
an ancient custom of Palestinian men. Instead of
using their own names, men addressed each other
as *abu,* which means "father of." The next name
would be either the name of their real-life son, a
relative, or a revered Arab hero. Yasir Arafat, who
had no children, became Abu Ammar, after an early
Islamic martyr named Ammar whose own father's
name was Yasir. Khalil Wazir became Abu Jihad.
Salah Khalaf became Abu Iyad. They were to use
these names for many years. Many Palestinians still
think of Yasir Arafat as Abu Ammar.

The next step was to decide on a name for their
movement. Several were suggested and used, until
Arafat decided on the Palestine Liberation Move-

**Ahmed al-Shuqairi, the first
chairman of the PLO, at the
1967 Arab summit confer-
ence in Khartoum, Sudan.
Arafat considered Shuqairi
insufficiently militant and
criticized him for being a
member of the generation of
leaders who had lost Palestine to Israel.**

ment. The Arabic name was *Harakat al-Tahrir al-Watani al-Filastini*. The revolutionaries wanted to call it HTF for short, using the initials of the keywords to form an acronym, but HTF was pronounced *hataf*, which means "death" in Arabic. After some discussion, they decided that this was too discouraging a name, and reversed the initials to read FTH, or *fatah*, an Arabic word for "conquest." The movement then became known as al-Fatah, "the conquest," or just Fatah.

Fatah's founders spent 1958 recruiting new members, gathering their resources, and preparing to publish their newsletter. Arafat also fell in love again but broke off his engagement, saying he felt it would be unfair to ask a woman to share the hardship he knew he would be facing.

The first issue of Fatah's newsletter, *Our Palestine*, appeared in 1959. It was published in Beirut, Lebanon, and distributed through underground organizations to Palestinians in Lebanon, the Persian Gulf states, Europe, and the United States. Most of its readers were located in Egypt, Syria, and Jordan, where the publication was banned as inflammatory propaganda. Abu Jihad took charge of smuggling copies into these countries. When he and Arafat learned that some Palestinians were being beaten

Christian pilgrims celebrate Palm Sunday at the Church of the Holy Sepulcher in Jerusalem. Christians believe the church was built on the place where Jesus Christ was crucified and buried.

and tortured by the Egyptian and Syrian police for having copies of *Our Palestine*, they regarded it as a demonstration that Fatah was considered dangerous and important by the authorities, which in turn attracted new volunteers and support.

Forty monthly issues of *Our Palestine* appeared between 1959 and 1963. Its text was mostly crude propaganda, often written hurriedly in the print shop by Arafat and Abu Jihad to fill the necessary number of pages, but it kept the idea of Palestinian nationalism alive. As disseminated in *Our Palestine*, Fatah's message was that the liberation of Palestine was up to the Palestinians, who could no longer wait for the other Arab nations to solve their problems but must strike against Israel on their own. This political philosophy won the organization many followers, particularly among younger Palestinians. When publication stopped in 1963, Fatah had moved another step closer to armed struggle against Israel. Combat training was under way.

With support from the Soviet Union and other nations, the Algerian revolutionaries who had just won their war of independence against France set up training camps in the deserts of Algeria. Fatah members, many of them former students whom Arafat and Abu Jihad had recruited in West Germany in 1957, were sent to the camps in the early 1960s. There they learned combat techniques as well as how to make bombs, blow up bridges, and carry out propaganda campaigns. Another important product of the guerrilla camps was the growth of an international network of underground fighters and terrorists. The Palestinians met young men and women from Iran, Turkey, the Philippines, Ethiopia, West Germany, Italy, Spain, Japan, North Korea, Northern Ireland, and Latin America. These international contacts proved useful to Fatah and the PLO in later years.

In 1963, Arafat decided that the years of preparation were over. He gave up his job in Kuwait, sold his construction company, and moved to Syria, whose socialist Ba'athist government Arafat found more receptive to his ideas than Nasser, whom Arafat had taken to criticizing at every opportunity. The Ba'athist party constitution proclaimed its dedication to the sovereignty of the Arab homeland, which it defined as all the Arab nations where Arabic was spoken, including Palestine. Nasser was still the Arab world's most important leader, but Arafat had grown impatient with his unwillingness to challenge Israel again. Despite its insistence on independent action, pushing the Arab nations toward war with Israel remained an integral part of Fatah's strategy. Groups of Fatah fedayeen began to launch raids into Israel from bases in Syria and Jordan. At the same time, Fatah obtained permission from the Algerian government to open an office in Algiers. The office was called the Bureau de la Palestine and was run by Abu Jihad. Algeria thus became the first nation to officially recognize the Palestinian resistance movement.

Further recognition followed. In 1964 Arafat and Abu Jihad were invited to visit Beijing, the capital of the People's Republic of China, which served as an inspiration to many liberation movements because of the success of its own revolution in 1949. Although Arafat and Jihad returned home disappointed because they did not get the opportunity to meet Chinese revolutionaries Mao Zedong or Zhou Enlai and did not receive the weapons and money they had hoped for, the trip boosted Fatah's prestige among the many Palestinian groups.

Arafat was particularly concerned about the creation of the Palestine Liberation Organization, which in its initial stages was sponsored and heavily influenced by Nasser and, to a lesser extent, the other Arab leaders. The charter of the PLO, prepared for the January 1964 meeting of the Arab League, provided for the establishment of a Palestinian national congress or council (PNC) made up of representatives from various Palestinian groups. Although Arafat essentially agreed with the aims of the PLO as expressed in its charter, Abu Sa'ed (Khaland Hassian), Fatah's delegate to the first meeting of the PNC, held in East Jerusalem in May, confirmed his fears that the organization was controlled by Nasser and the other Arab League leaders and seemed to have been devised as a means of directing and placating the Palestinian nationalist movement. Arafat also opposed the PLO's first president, Ahmed Shuqairi. Although Shuqairi was a lawyer who had been active in Palestinian causes, an eloquent orator, and a diplomat who represented Saudi Arabia and later Syria before the UN, Arafat

Arab demonstrators picket in front of the White House in Washington, D.C., in late May 1967, just prior to the beginning of the Six-Day War. The United States was often the focus of Arab resentment because of the large amount of financial and military aid the country provided Israel.

A 1963 photograph of a Bedouin campsite. The Bedouins are nomadic Arab herdsmen and traders. Within Israel most live in the Negev Desert, where the Israeli government has sought to confine them to small agricultural plots. Cultural differences between Bedouins and the more sedentary Palestinians contributed to the friction in Jordan in the early 1970s.

believed he was compromised by his ties to Nasser. Shuqairi was also older than Arafat and Fatah's other leaders, and in Arafat's mind this linked him to the leaders, like Haj Amin, who had lost Palestine, called by Arafat the "generation of disgrace."

Arafat did not publicly denounce the PLO, but he and Fatah had little to do with it. Nevertheless, many Palestinians were pleased to have an openly acknowledged representative organization with offices in Cairo and some of the trappings of a legitimate government. More than anything else, the PLO and Fatah provided the Palestinians with a psychological lift. Many of the displaced Palestinians, particularly those in the refugee camps, felt powerless to affect their own fate. The activities of Fatah and the PLO demonstrated that the Palestinians did not have to resign themselves to being the passive victims of Middle Eastern politics but could act themselves to accomplish their goals. Although Fatah lost some members to the PLO, Arafat and his fedayeen carried on with their grim work, attacking Israeli settlements and installations and then retreating across the border into the hills of Syria and Jordan.

The guerrilla raids ensured a constant level of tension between Israel and its neighbors. At the same time, Syria's support for Fatah and its shelling of

Israeli settlements from the strategic Golan Heights enabled it to take a leadership role in the Middle East. Not wishing Syria to appear more committed to Arab nationalism than Egypt, Nasser challenged Israel by massing troops on its border and closing the Strait of Tiran to Israeli shipping. Syria also mobilized its troops. Severely outnumbered and convinced that war was unavoidable, Israel decided to strike the first blow in June 1967 by attacking Egyptian airfields. The grounded Egyptian air force was almost entirely destroyed, and Israeli ground forces routed their stunned Egyptian and Syrian counterparts. Jordan's King Hussein had no love for either Nasser or the Syrian government, but he was deceived by Nasser's reports of early Egyptian victories and believed Jordan ought to play a part in the Arab triumph. The Jordanian forces were mauled. The war lasted just six days and ended in one of the most one-sided victories of modern times. Israel added the Gaza Strip, the Sinai Peninsula, the Golan Heights, and the West Bank to its territory. Among the captured territory was East Jerusalem, known as the Old City, home to the most sacred sites of Judaism, Christianity, and Islam. A famous photograph shows Israeli soldiers crying at the Wailing Wall, but many Arabs also wept at the loss of their holy places.

> *Out of the ashes of this disastrous war will arise the phoenix of a free Arab Palestine.*
> —YASIR ARAFAT
> on the Six-Day War

Arafat was able to turn the Arab defeat to Fatah's benefit. The PLO, which was closely associated with Arab governments, lost prestige. Many Palestinians were disgusted that PLO forces had played no part in the war. Arafat stepped up Fatah's raids on Israel, reinforcing Fatah's image as the militant arm of the PLO. Less than a year later Israel decided to smash the guerrilla bases in Jordan, and Arafat became the hero of Karameh. He took advantage of the attention he received after Karameh to increase Fatah's influence, at the expense of Shuqairi. By the time the PNC met in Cairo in February 1969, most delegates looked to Arafat and Fatah as the saviors of Palestine. Leaders of the various groups and communities represented in the PNC persuaded the Arab League that Shuqairi had to go. Arafat was elected chairman of the PLO, and Fatah became the most powerful element in the group. Nasser and Arafat agreed to forget their past differences and embraced one another.

Fatah gained hundreds of new fedayeen. Arafat found his most fertile recruiting ground in the dozens of Palestinian refugee camps. Israel's victory in the Six-Day War created a new generation of displaced Palestinians, and new camps sprang up in Lebanon, Syria, Egypt, and Jordan. The Palestinians lived in tents and cinder-block homes and were provided with food and aid by the United Nations Relief and Works Agency for Palestine Refugees in the Near East (UNRWA). By 1968 there were an estimated 1.7 million Palestinians in the camps. The poverty and suffering found there led the PLO to compare them to the ghettos of Europe in which the Jews had been segregated at various times during the diaspora. The hardship also bred the fighters who carried on the war with Israel. United by history, kinship, and the memory of their lost homeland, the Palestinians in the camps kept the dream of Palestinian nationalism alive.

PLO gunmen take cover during the street fighting in Amman, Jordan, in September 1970. Believing that the PLO presence was undermining his authority, Jordan's King Hussein ordered his army to drive the organization from the country. Palestinians refer to that month as Black September.

Arafat's successes were followed by tragedy. The PLO established a stronghold in Jordan where they used villages and the camps to launch attacks on Israel. This did not sit well with Hussein and the Jordanian people, who stood to suffer from Israeli retaliation. The situation was aggravated by the traditional enmity between Jordan's nomadic Bedouin majority and the Palestinians, most of whom had been town and city dwellers. In addition, the PLO conducted itself as a separate government within Jordan, collecting its own taxes, conducting its own courts, and operating its own offices in Amman. Armed fedayeen promenaded through Amman's streets, and in June 1970 fedayeen attempted to assassinate Hussein. The powerlessness of the Jordanian government was demonstrated in early September 1970, when guerrillas loyal to the Popular Front for the Liberation of Palestine (PFLP), a faction within the PLO, hijacked three Western planes, landed them in the Jordanian desert, and refused to negotiate with Jordanian officials. Two weeks later Hussein declared war on the PLO. Syria initially sent troops to the PLO's aid but withdrew when Israel threatened to intervene. The fighting lasted for several weeks, ending only when Nasser was able to mediate between Arafat and Hussein. Five thousand Palestinians were killed; thousands more were wounded. Black September, as the Palestinians refer to it, also claimed Nasser as a victim. After concluding negotiations between Arafat and Hussein, the exhausted Egyptian president suffered a fatal heart attack.

By the beginning of 1971 the PLO had been driven out of Jordan into Syria and Lebanon. Arafat was forbidden to enter the country he had thought of as his base of operations. He set up a new headquarters in Lebanon and began to plan the PLO's next step.

5

The Terror Weapon

In the minds of many people, particularly in the West, the PLO is most immediately associated with terrorism. Hijackings, bombings, kidnappings, and shootings have been directed at civilian targets by Palestinians who claim that their actions are desperate political statements. Not all of these terrorists have been acting on Arafat's orders, although most of them have been associated with the PLO in some way.

Under Arafat's leadership the PLO quickly changed from a single body to a loose confederation of separate groups, each with its own leaders. Arafat has compared the PLO to a big tent; it holds many Palestinians, he says, but they are not all members of the same family. Such a structure enables all the different guerrilla and nationalist groups, despite differences in tactics and ideology, to work together for the common cause of a liberated Palestine.

Fatah has been the largest group in the PLO since 1969. Its membership is a closely guarded secret, but most expert observers say that it probably has about 10,000 members. Since 1971 Arafat has been the commander in chief of the PLO's Revolutionary Forces, which are made up of the fedayeen of all the

Armed struggle is the only way to liberate Palestine. Thus it is the overall strategy, not merely a tactical phase.
—the Palestinian National Charter

A member of the Palestinian Liberation Army (PLA) instructs a young Palestinian on the use of firearms in April 1969. The PLA was established in the mid-1960s by the executive committee of the PLO. Its members were recruited from the Palestinian populations of Syria, Jordan, Lebanon, and other Arab countries.

PLO subgroups. In 1973 he was made head of the group's political department, meaning that he is the PLO representative responsible for international affairs. Fatah's biggest backer among the Arab nations is Saudi Arabia, which gives Arafat several million dollars each year for weapons and other expenses.

The second largest PLO subgroup is the Popular Front for the Liberation of Palestine (PFLP), with an estimated 3,500 members. It was founded in 1967 by George Habash, a Palestinian who was educated as a physician in Beirut. Habash was the political leader of a revolutionary group that drove the British out of the Arab states of Aden and southern Arabia in the late 1960s. The PFLP is a Marxist organization that wants to overthrow not just Israel but also conservative Arab regimes such as the Saudi Arabian monarchy. Arafat's followers and Ha-

PLA instructors teach fedayeen recruits how to use land mines. The PLA received funds from the nations of the Arab League — who generally provided less money than they pledged — and from taxes collected by the PLO.

bash's have frequently disagreed on such matters as long-term goals, how much violence is justified to achieve those goals, and whether to cooperate with the Arab governments. Habash preaches a gospel of constant revolutionary violence until the Middle East is liberated under Marxist principles.

The Popular Democratic Front for the Liberation of Palestine (PDFLP) is a splinter group that broke away from Habash's organization in 1969. Led by Nayef Hawatmeh, a Jordanian Christian, the PDFLP's 500 or so members are especially critical of Hussein for not engaging in constant war with Israel. The PDFLP has ties with the Soviet Union, from which it receives money and guns.

Another very militant splinter group of the PFLP is the Popular Front for the Liberation of Palestine —General Command (PFLP—GC). Its approximately 150 members are all hard-core guerrilla commandos. The GC is led by Ahmed Jabril, who was once an officer in the Syrian army.

Stewards aboard a Swissair jet hijacked by PLO commandos in September 1970 distribute food to passengers. At the time the photograph was taken the PLO was also holding two other hijacked airliners and their passengers in the desert near Amman.

The PLO gunmen released the passengers from the three airliners hijacked in September 1970 before blowing up the planes. The hijackings and the refusal of the PLO to negotiate with the Jordanian government were a great embarrassment to Hussein and triggered Black September.

As-Saiga (the Thunderbolt) was established by the Syrian government in 1967. Although part of the PLO, it is funded mostly by Syria and has close ties to the Syrian army. Led by Zuheir Mohsen, it has about 1,500 men, but the group is involved more in politics than in guerrilla operations.

The Arab Liberation Front (ALF) is made up of about 100 Palestinians who are linked to the Ba'ath religious and political party in Iraq. Led by Abdel Wahab Kayyali and funded by Iraq, its members seldom take part in either fighting or politics. One PLO official said of the ALF that its main purpose appears to be to keep an eye on the other groups.

The Arab National Youth Organization for the Liberation of Palestine (ANYOLP) may no longer exist. During the early 1970s it was backed by Libya's leader, Muammar al-Qaddafi, and specialized in international hijackings. ANYOLP defied Arafat's orders on several occasions and has not been heard of since the late 1970s. Its members were probably killed or taken into other groups.

This cluster of organizations made up Arafat's PLO in the early 1970s. During that time the PLO and its subgroups stepped up their border raids into Israel. They also sought to export the war of liberation by directing attacks against people and

property in the rest of the world in order to call attention to their cause and provoke a response from the Western powers.

After the Six-Day War of 1967, the Palestinians utilized three types of terrorist activity. One was the artillery bombardment of Israeli settlements from across the borders of neighboring countries. Another was the infiltration of Israel by agents who planted bombs in nightclubs, restaurants, and other public places and attacked settlers on the West Bank, referred to in Israel by the biblical names Judea and Samaria. The third was the exportation of terror into other countries by the hijacking of airplanes and the planting of bombs. Although the victims of international terror were sometimes Israeli diplomats or tourists, more often those affected were individuals who happened to be in the wrong place at the wrong time.

The first act of international terror by the PLO was the 1968 hijacking of an Israeli plane by PFLP commandos who forced the pilot to fly the plane to Algeria. All of the passengers were finally released. The PFLP hijacking in September 1970 of three Western airliners — British, Swiss, and American — that led to Hussein's war with the PLO was one of the most spectacular terrorist actions. The planes

Israeli military personnel secure a section of Lod International Airport in Tel Aviv minutes after 3 Japanese gunmen killed 27 people there in May 1972. The three were members of a radical Japanese organization with close ties to a PLO group.

were taken to a remote location in the Jordanian desert. After several weeks the passengers were released, and the jets were blown up.

In February 1972 the PFLP hijacked a West German plane and collected $5 million in ransom for the passengers and crew. Three months later 3 Japanese "tourists" pulled out guns at Lod Airport in the Israeli city of Tel Aviv and slaughtered 27 people. Two of the Japanese gunmen were killed in the assault, and the third was captured. He told the Israeli authorities that the three were members of a Japanese underground group called the Army of the Red Star and had been recruited by the PFLP to carry out the operation.

The PDFLP's most notorious exploit was a raid on the Israeli settlement of Ma'alot in May 1974. The terrorists seized a school and held the children hostage. The captors were eventually killed by Israeli forces, but not before 21 schoolchildren were murdered. In a similar raid on the Qiryat Shimona settlement by the PFLP — GC that same year, 16 Israelis were killed.

Perhaps the most infamous terrorist action was carried out by the Black September faction of Fatah, organized by Abu Iyad (Salah Khalaf). It announced its presence with the Cairo assassination of Waifi

Tal, a Jordanian diplomat, and Hussein's chief adviser, in November 1971. Nearly a year later, in September 1972, 8 Black Septembrists, clad in sports clothes and ski masks, took 11 Israeli athletes hostage at the Olympic Games in Munich, West Germany. Two Israeli athletes were killed resisting the commandos. The captors demanded the release of 200 Palestinian prisoners from Israeli jails in exchange for the athletes' freedom. After almost 20 hours of bargaining with West German authorities, the Palestinians were persuaded to move from the dormitory to a nearby military airport, where a jet was to take them to Cairo. At the airport a shootout took place, and the nine Israelis, as well as six of the commandos, were killed. The surviving Black Septembrists were released the following month when other members of the group hijacked a West German jet and took its passengers hostage, agreeing to free them only in exchange for the release of the Palestinians being held for the Munich murders.

In March 1973 eight Black Septembrists took over the Saudi Arabian embassy in Khartoum, the capital of Sudan. They held American, Saudi, Jordanian, and Belgian diplomats hostage. When the Jordanian government refused to release 17 Black

A masked Palestinian guerrilla peers from an athletic dormitory at the Olympic Games in Munich, West Germany, where members of the Black September organization took Israeli athletes hostage in September 1972. Following negotiations, nine athletes and six guerrillas died in a shootout at a nearby airport.

September prisoners, the American and the 2 Belgians were machine-gunned to death in a basement room.

In July 1976 Palestinian commandos claiming to be members of the PFLP (Habash later denied that they were members of his group) hijacked an Air France plane bound from Tel Aviv, Israel, to Paris, France, and forced the pilot to fly to Entebbe Airport in Uganda. The hijackers released more than 100 of their hostages but held 90 or so Jewish passengers, demanding the release of political prisoners in Israel and elsewhere in exchange. A specially trained Israeli counterterrorist strike force flew to Entebbe and rescued most of the hostages (three were killed in the crossfire). All of the hijackers died during the rescue.

The incidents recounted compose just a short list of some of the more highly publicized and spectacular of the PLO's terrorist activities. The PLO also attempted hijackings and other major operations in Italy, Greece, Switzerland, Belgium, the Netherlands, Paraguay, India, France, Canada, Argentina, Zaire, Cyprus, Spain, the United States, Thailand,

This bus was set afire in a battle between Israeli troops and Palestinian hijackers on the Tel Aviv–Haifa highway in March 1978. Terrorism succeeded in drawing attention to the Palestinian cause, but because its victims were often civilians, it also earned the Palestinians much condemnation.

and most of the Arab nations between 1968 and 1976. The most frequent target, of course, was Israel, where numerous attacks and bombings on markets took place.

The most common rationale for terrorism is that it focuses attention on a problem that would otherwise be ignored or overlooked. The Palestinians argue that given their stateless existence and Israel's military might, terrorism is one of the few means available to them for striking at Israel. The citizens and property of nations other than Israel were targeted to demonstrate that the support of their government enabled Israel to carry out its policies. By attacking Israel's allies, the PLO hoped to make such support costly in human and material terms. Even Arab governments and officials that the PLO deemed insufficiently committed to the Palestinians have had operations directed at them. Although Fatah's strategy of terrorism undoubtedly kept the world aware of the Palestinian situation, it also earned the PLO widespread condemnation, as many governments and individuals criticized Fatah and other groups for making civilians the targets of their attacks.

Fatah's response was that it was Palestinian civilians who had been and continued to be the targets of Israeli policy. It was Palestinian civilians who had been displaced by Israel's creation, who had lost their homes during Israel's war of independence, who lived under Israeli military occupation on the West Bank, and who often suffered the consequences of Israel's reprisal raids on their villages and camps. Israeli bombers often hit the refugee camps in retaliation for PLO attacks, and the bombs made no distinction between civilians and fedayeen. After Menachem Begin became Israel's prime minister in 1977, Israel's policy toward the West Bank changed. In the years following the Six-Day War, Israel had been uncertain as to the West Bank's ultimate disposition. Begin encouraged a policy of Israeli settlement on the West Bank and asserted that because Judea and Samaria were traditionally part of the Promised Land, Israel would never relinquish them. Palestinians saw in the West Bank sce-

The only surviving member of the three-man Japanese group that carried out the Lod Airport massacre in 1972 stood trial in Israel. He confirmed that the attack had been ordered by the Popular Front for the Liberation of Palestine (PFLP), a PLO group headed by George Habash.

Arafat, George Habash of the PFLP, and Nayef Hawatmeh of the Popular Democratic Front for the Liberation of Palestine (PDFLP) at a meeting of the Palestinian National Congress in Algiers, Algeria, in 1983. Over the years Algeria was a consistent supporter of the PLO.

nario a repetition of the loss of their original lands. Israeli settlers on the West Bank were fair game for Arab attack because they were serving to carry out Israeli government policy that would ultimately, the PLO believed, displace hundreds of thousands more Palestinians. General Ariel Sharon, minister of defense and agriculture under Begin, acknowledged that the settlers were helping to achieve Israel's security interest. "Security is not only guns and aircraft and tanks," he said. "Security is first of all motivation — motivation to defend a place. If people live in a place, they have the motivation to defend themselves, and the nation has the motivation to defend them."

Without an air force or a standing army, the PLO carried on the war with Israel in what it believed was the only method left to it. Negotiation was dismissed as ineffective. Just as the Arab nations steadfastly refused to acknowledge Israel's right to exist, Israel consistently refused to accept or negotiate with the PLO. Golda Meir, Israel's prime minister from 1969 to 1974, even went so far as to say that the Palestinians did not exist. The Palestinians believe that Israel's intransigence is the more reprehensible, as the Palestinians have already been deprived of their land and homes and exist only as a displaced or occupied people.

Arafat's public stance toward terrorism has evolved. There is little doubt that during the 1970s Fatah espoused and directed terrorist operations. The notorious Black September group was almost certainly under Fatah's direction, but Abu Iyad (Salah Khalef), Black September's organizer, said that Arafat had little choice but to advocate such radical tactics if he wished to maintain control of the PLO, whose membership was demanding a more militant stance. In recent years Fatah spokesmen have tried to sidestep the issue of terrorism and have asserted that the PLO is attempting to use other methods to regain Palestine. Fatah's official line is that terrorism is to be used only as a last resort. It should be remembered that "terrorist" is a relative term. Those denounced as terrorists are often revered as freedom fighters by their own side and sometimes

regarded as statesmen and leaders once their goals have been achieved. Both Menachem Begin and Anwar Sadat, Egypt's president from 1970 to 1981 and the first Arab leader to sign a peace treaty with Israel, were at one time terrorists. Those PLO members denounced as terrorists by the West are acclaimed as brave fedayeen by their compatriots. The danger and tragedy of the Israeli-Palestinian conflict is that the violence, passed to new generations, hardening attitudes on both sides, has now been escalating the cycle of retaliation as more blood is shed. Each side loses the ability to see the other as individuals, leaving both unable to compromise, for to do so would betray the sacrifices of those who went before. What is left, in the words of a retired Israeli army commander quoted by David Shipler in his perceptive study *Arab and Jew*, is a "vicious circle, blood for blood, and at the end you cannot remember where was the beginning. And you are not more than just the other side."

PLO guerrillas on patrol in southern Lebanon in 1979. After it was driven from Jordan in 1970, the PLO soon established a stronghold in Lebanon, where the ongoing conflict between Muslims and Christians and the weakness of the government enabled the organization to operate freely.

6

"The Winds of Paradise"

Between 1969 and 1973 the PLO continued its guerrilla attacks along Israel's borders and carried out hijackings and other operations. While continuing to emphasize that Palestinians must act to liberate themselves, Arafat and the PLO leaders still hoped that a new full-scale war between Israel and the Arab states would liberate territory for the Palestinians. During the same period Egypt and Israel engaged in what has since been called the War of Attrition, characterized by skirmishes along the Suez Canal, commando raids into each other's territory, and Israeli air attacks on Egyptian cities.

In October 1973 Egypt, Iraq, and Syria attacked Israel in the hope of regaining some of the territory the Israelis had seized in the Six-Day War. Although Egypt did regain much of the Sinai Peninsula, the October, or Yom Kippur, War — so called by the Israelis because Egypt attacked on the Jewish holy day of Yom Kippur — was not the Arab victory the PLO had been waiting for. Egypt had to agree to reduce the size of its forces along the Suez Canal, and Syria did not regain an inch of the Golan Heights. None of the former territory of Palestine was regained, and the PLO did not participate directly in the fighting or in the peace negotiations.

It was, in fact, the Yom Kippur war that saved the PLO from probable extinction, and which gave Arafat the opportunity to continue its struggle by political means.
—ALAN HART
English historian
and biographer

Arafat gives the victory sign. During the 1970s Arafat emphasized diplomatic initiatives, hoping to win wider recognition and support for the PLO. The high point of these efforts came when he was invited to address the UN in 1974.

The setback confirmed Arafat's growing belief that it was unrealistic, perhaps impossible, to expect to liberate Palestine by force of arms alone. Israel was simply too strong, and the massive amount of aid it received from the United States made it more formidable still. Arafat now began to emphasize diplomatic measures as a means of achieving international recognition for the PLO. Although he remained an impassioned and spellbinding orator capable of fiery, militant rhetoric on public occasions, in private he hinted that he would be willing to negotiate with Israel. The PLO's official policy insisted upon the complete dismantlement of the state of Israel and the return of all of Palestine to Arab control, but after 25 years of fighting Arafat appeared willing to admit that a Palestinian homeland, perhaps in the Gaza Strip and the West Bank, might be able to coexist with Israel.

Arafat's new diplomacy did not mean that the PLO would abandon the military struggle, only that it would also work for acknowledgment as a legitimate political organization. While the fedayeen continued their border attacks from Lebanon and Syria, Arafat lobbied world leaders for their support. In October 1974 the UN invited the PLO to participate in a debate on Palestine and the Middle East that was to take place the following month. (Israel and the United States had voted against including the PLO in the debate but had been outvoted.) Arafat accepted the invitation. One week later France's foreign minister met with Arafat in Beirut. It was Arafat's first official meeting with a Western diplomat, and it conferred on him something of the status of a statesman.

Arafat's prestige received another boost a few days later in Rabat, the capital of Morocco, at a meeting of the heads of state of the Arab nations. There they voted to recognize the PLO as "the sole legitimate representative of the Palestinian people" and Arafat as its spokesman. Hussein, who had claimed the right to negotiate for those Palestinians living on the West Bank, conceded that privilege to the PLO. The new decision meant that the Arab leaders considered Arafat to be just as much a statesman as

We Arabs did not kill 6 million Jews or persecute them. Europeans did that. But we Arabs paid the price. I think I'm entitled to say that life has not been very fair to us.

—YASIR ARAFAT

King Faisal of Saudi Arabia or President Sadat of Egypt. More importantly, it was also a declaration by the Arab nations that no international settlement of territorial disputes in the Middle East could take place without the PLO's participation. Sobbing, Arafat told the assembled Arab dignitaries, "This summit conference has been like a wedding feast for the Palestinians." He then returned to his headquarters in Beirut to prepare for his forthcoming UN speech.

Arafat's arrival in New York City kicked off a wave of threats and demonstrations. Angry that the UN was honoring a man whom they considered a terrorist, members of Jewish groups paraded in front of the UN buildings. More than 1,000 police were assigned to protect the PLO leader and his aides.

The visit went smoothly, reaching its high point on November 13, when Arafat addressed the UN General Assembly, which consists of the representatives of all the member nations. (He chose to stand beside the chair customarily provided for a head of state.) The Arafat who appeared on newspaper front pages and television screens all over the world that

Almost 25,000 people gathered outside the United Nations buildings in New York City in November 1974 to protest the appearance of Arafat before the General Assembly. Israeli politicians Abba Eban and Moshe Dayan addressed the crowd of demonstrators.

PALESTINE
IS
MY
HOMELAND

.O.
presents the
Palestinians and
ir Struggle for
Sdetermination

WELCOME
P.L.O.

Palestinians and their supporters welcomed Arafat to
the UN. The press reported
that the security measures
employed by the UN during
Arafat's visit were unprecedented in the history of the
international peacekeeping
organization.

day was a striking figure. He had shaved off his
characteristic stubble and removed his dark
glasses, but he still wore his checkered kaffiyeh. At
his hip, prominently displayed as he stood before
the nations of the world, was a large black holster.

The holster was empty. For security reasons, Arafat was not permitted to carry a gun into the General Assembly, but he insisted on wearing the
holster. "Everyone must see that I have had to fight
to get here," he told an aide.

The UN before which Arafat appeared in 1974 was
a very different organization from the one that had
voted to partition Palestine in 1947. Many new nations had been created in the intervening 27 years,
and the UN's membership had increased corre-
spondingly. Many of the new nations — especially
Third World countries in Africa, Asia, and Latin
America — had won their independence through revolution. Their leaders were more likely to view Arafat
as a freedom fighter than as a terrorist and were
willing to recognize him as a fellow statesman. Many
of them were already sympathetic to his cause. The
Israelis, of course, objected to Arafat's presence at
the UN, and the Israeli delegation did not attend his
speech.

Arafat's 80-minute speech was his version of the
Palestinian story. Although well delivered, it con-
tained no new ideas and simply repeated earlier
public statements about the Palestinians' rights to
a homeland, but its conclusion was stirring. With
arms spread toward his audience, Arafat said, "Today I have come bearing an olive branch and a freedom fighter's gun. Do not let the olive branch fall
from my hand. I repeat: Do not let the olive branch
fall from my hand." (The olive branch is a traditional
symbol of peace.)

As Arafat left the podium, he clasped his hands
over his head in a boxer's victory gesture. He was
answered with a roar of applause, led by the delegates of the Arab nations. (The United States delegation, under instruction to avoid giving the
appearance of taking sides, did not applaud.)

The cheers Arafat received in the General Assembly were echoed by PLO supporters around the

world. Arafat's speech was beamed to the Arab world by satellite and was heard by millions. In the streets of Beirut and Cairo, excited crowds gathered around anyone who had a transistor radio. Schools and other services were closed in the Palestinian refugee camps, and the day was declared a Palestinian national holiday. The next day's issue of the Lebanese newspaper *An Nahar* featured a cartoon in which a smiling world tipped its hat to Arafat.

At the UN, Israeli delegate Yosef Tekoah followed Arafat's speech by lambasting the organization for "prostrating itself" before the PLO, which was guilty of the "premeditated murder of innocent civilians." Tekoah's angry speech did not make as big a stir as Arafat's had because most of the Third World delegates walked out on it.

After his heady moment in the UN limelight, Arafat set off on a series of goodwill tours, visiting Cuba, Algeria, Saudi Arabia, Libya, Egypt, Yugoslavia, and the Soviet Union. He was photographed and interviewed for hundreds of magazines and newspapers. A U.S. magazine dubbed him "one of the most intriguing people of the year." Although Arafat became something of a guerrilla celebrity and opened many doors that had been previously closed to the PLO, the United States did not officially recognize the organization.

For the most part, Arafat's speech to the UN General Assembly — in which he said that he came bearing both a freedom fighter's gun and the olive branch of peace — was well received by the delegates, although the Israeli delegation walked out.

U.S. secretary of state Henry Kissinger was determined to limit the influence of the Soviet Union and its allies in the Middle East by forging a peace agreement between the region's two most powerful nations, Israel and Egypt. Other Arab nations bitterly criticized Egypt for considering a separate peace with Israel. Unwavering opposition to Israel's right to exist had been the foundation for what little Arab unity existed, but Sadat believed Egypt could no longer bear the high cost of continued hostility. His nation was exceedingly poor, and funds that were needed for internal development were instead spent on war and the military. Under Sadat, Egypt had broken with the Soviet Union, and the country was desperate for the amount and type of aid that only the United States could provide. Kissinger succeeded in getting Israel and Egypt to agree on such issues as ownership of the Sinai Peninsula and control of the Gaza Strip. A series of partial agreements was signed. The peace initiative continued under U.S. president Jimmy Carter, who was elected in 1976. When Sadat flew to Jerusalem in November

Sadat (left), U.S. president Jimmy Carter (center), and Israeli prime minister Menachem Begin (right) sign the Egyptian-Israeli peace treaty known as the Camp David accord in March 1979. Carter's personal diplomacy was essential to reaching an agreement.

1977 to address the Knesset, the Israeli parliament, it was as historic and unprecedented an occasion as Arafat's visit to the United Nations had been. After a series of meetings with Carter, Sadat and Begin signed a peace treaty in March 1979. Its most obvious result was the return of the Sinai Peninsula to Egyptian control. The West Bank, Gaza Strip, and Golan Heights remained unaffected. The outraged Palestinians felt that Sadat had sold out the Arab cause for peace with a powerful neighbor and U.S. dollars.

Arafat continued to work on achieving recognition for the PLO. He met with Austrian chancellor Bruno Kreisky and with West German, Spanish, Portuguese, and Iranian officials. Arafat's diplomacy cost the PLO the support of Libyan strongman Muammar al-Qaddafi, who felt that Arafat was growing too moderate, but the breach between the two helped Arafat's image, as Qaddafi was unpopular in both the Middle East and the West. In 1980 the European Economic Community (sometimes called the Common Market) announced that its member nations believed the PLO should be included in any international peace talks about the Middle East.

In the late 1970s the PLO's fedayeen in Lebanon stepped up their guerrilla activity on Israel's northern border. Raids and rocket fire from PLO bases in Lebanon provoked a series of increasingly bitter counterattacks by the Israeli Defense Forces, and by the early 1980s Israel was ready to act to remove the PLO from Lebanon. For the first time the PLO found itself in prolonged, direct combat with Israel. The presence of PLO fighters in Lebanon was only one of many problems in that troubled country. Lebanon had experienced ongoing civil strife and bloodshed since 1975. Its constitution called for proportional representation in the nation's government based on the population of the country's various religious groups. The Maronite Christians dominated the government, as they had for years, but by the 1970s the Muslims were in the majority. Because the last census had been taken in 1932, the Muslims were denied fair representation. Civil war between the Muslims and Christians resulted.

Arafat with Indira Gandhi, then prime minister of India, in 1983. By the 1980s the PLO had taken on many of the characteristics of a government, with diplomatic representatives in many nations, but it still lacked a state.

Complicating the situation was the presence of the PLO. The Christian government opposed the PLO's growing independence in Lebanon, and the Muslims opposed any attempt by the government to rein in the PLO. Israel supported the Christians and regularly struck against PLO bases in the southern part of the country.

In 1976 a fifth force entered the picture when the Arab League asked Syria's president Hafez al-Assad to send peacekeeping troops into Lebanon. Assad was happy to comply with this request because he wanted to gain influence in the Middle East. By maintaining troops in Lebanon, he believed, he could keep any one group from gaining power there. With Lebanon weak and divided, the country's leaders would depend on Syria for help, and Assad's importance would be increased. Arafat and the PLO had meanwhile used the turmoil in Lebanon to begin the establishment of their own governmental infrastructure in West Beirut and southern Lebanon and opposed the Syrian intervention. Skirmishes between the Syrians and the PLO ensued, and Assad made several attempts to seize control of the PLO.

A wounded guerrilla is carried by Israeli soldiers who intercepted a PLO raiding party that had landed on Nahariya Beach, Galilee, in April 1979. The PLO used southern Lebanon as a staging ground for attacks on Israel during the 1970s and 1980s.

After 1976 border incidents between PLO guerrillas and Israelis increased. The Israelis had built many settlements in Galilee, and fedayeen based in southern Lebanon made them the target of frequent rocket attacks and night raids. So many PLO members were located in Lebanon, especially in the south, that they called the region "Fatahland."

Although the Lebanese had welcomed the Palestinians as fellow Arabs in 1971, they paid a high price for their hospitality. Israeli jets and gunboats frequently sent rockets and artillery shells into Lebanese residential communities, and many Lebanese were killed. When the PLO accused Israel of murdering civilians, the Israelis replied that it was the PLO's fault for deliberately locating their bases in civilian areas. Through the late 1970s and into the 1980s, the pattern of attack, counterattack, and retaliation went on.

In June 1982 Israel launched Operation Peace for Galilee, a full-scale invasion of Lebanon. The stated purpose was to drive the fedayeen from their bases in southern Lebanon, but guerrilla activity there had greatly diminished after a cease-fire had gone into effect nearly a year earlier. From the outset Israel's goal was West Beirut, more than 50 miles north of the border, where the PLO had made its headquarters. Israel hoped to either destroy the PLO or drive it from the Middle East and in so doing eliminate its influence as a source of nationalist agitation on the West Bank, where the Palestinians outnumbered Israeli settlers by 750,000 to 30,000. As the well-armed IDF advanced toward Beirut it destroyed 7 refugee camps, more than 100,000 homes, and all the schools and clinics established by the UNRWA over the previous 32 years. More than 600,000 Palestinians and Lebanese were left homeless; 20,000 were killed. Israeli bombers flew ahead and attacked West Beirut, softening that part of the city for the pending assault. When Syria attempted to send forces to aid the PLO, the Israeli air force shot down 92 Syrian jets, and Assad withdrew his support.

The Israeli advance halted at West Beirut, the Muslim section of Lebanon's divided capital city.

Hafez al-Assad of Syria came to power in November 1970. Seeking preeminence in the Arab world, Assad received Arab League permission to intervene in the fighting between Muslims and Christians in Lebanon.

A Palestinian woman laments the September 1982 massacre of civilians in the Sabra and Shatila refugee camps in West Beirut. The killing was done by Lebanese Christian militiamen, with the tacit approval of the Israeli military.

The IDF troops consisted of 90,000 men, compared to only 15,000 PLO fighters, but the PLO forces were well entrenched among the area's nearly 500,000 inhabitants. Unwilling to engage in the kind of savage, hand-to-hand combat necessary to roust the fedayeen from the city's streets, buildings, and alleyways, the IDF decided on a siege. It surrounded West Beirut on three sides, leaving the Mediterranean Sea as the PLO's only route of escape. The IDF imposed a total blockade on West Beirut. Electricity and water were shut off. Food, fuel, and medical supplies were interdicted. Medical personnel were forbidden to enter. Israeli artillery and bombers unleashed a constant barrage, making no distinction between civilian and military targets. Four out of West Beirut's five hospitals suffered severe damage from the bombardment, and one, Gaza Hospital, was declared a military target by Israel and had to be evacuated.

The siege lasted 67 days. The Israelis made repeated efforts to pin down Arafat's location so that they could bomb it. They also hoped to find and kill Abu Iyad (Salah Khalaf), George Habash, and Abu Jihad (Khalil Wazir). Shortly after the siege began, Abu Iyad discovered that the Israelis had planted about 30 double agents in the PLO. These agents carried small radio transmitters and were supposed to broadcast Arafat's location to the waiting IDF bombers. Abu Iyad had the agents executed.

At one point in August, the Israelis seemed poised to make a final assault. Remembering that day, Arafat said that he prayed for 30 minutes, then told his staff members, "I feel the winds of paradise are blowing," meaning that he believed his time to die had arrived and that he would be rewarded with paradise for dying as a martyr for his cause. He urged his forces to meet the assault with bravery. Cheering and shouting "the winds of paradise are blowing," the PLO troops lined up shoulder to shoulder, prepared to face the assault of the IDF tanks, but the Israelis did not advance. They merely tightened the noose around West Beirut and waited.

After more than nine weeks Arafat admitted defeat. Under the terms of an agreement negotiated by U.S. special envoy Philip Habib, Arafat agreed to withdraw the PLO from Lebanon, Israel agreed not to send its troops into West Beirut, and the United States guaranteed the safety of the remaining 500,000 Palestinians in Lebanon. The UN sent a peacekeeping force of soldiers from several nations to Beirut to oversee the PLO's evacuation. Ships would carry the surviving fedayeen, about 8,000 in number, to Tunisia, Sudan, and Yemen. In a final show of defiance, the fedayeen fired their weapons into the air as the ships left the harbor. Arafat went first to Greece and then to Tunisia, where he planned to set up a new headquarters in the capital city of Tunis.

The withdrawal of the PLO did not bring an end to conflict in Lebanon. In September IDF officers allowed their allies in the Lebanese Christian militia forces to enter the Sabra and Shatila Palestinian refugee camps. Israel subsequently claimed that there were 2,000 terrorists in the camps, but investigatory commissions concluded that Israel knew that no fedayeen remained. Two days before the militias entered the camps, newly elected president Bashir Gemayel, a Christian, had been assassinated, and his brother Amin had called for the Christians to avenge his death. Israeli soldiers stood by outside the camps while the Christian militiamen massacred the residents. Israeli flares provided light for the slaughter; afterward the militias borrowed Israeli tanks to raze the camps' houses. Many of the dead were interred in the rubble. An international investigatory committee concluded that the militias had met with no resistance from the camps' inhabitants. Many of the dead were women and children. The total number killed was a matter of controversy. The Western and Israeli press initially reported 300, then 800; Lebanese sources say more than 2,000 were killed, and that the earlier, lower figures were only those counted by the Red Cross, who had overlooked the many bodies either lost in the rubble or carried away by relatives for burial. Arafat cites a figure of 3,200 dead, which concurs with the count of Amon Kapeliouke, an Israeli journalist. The incident was denounced all over

A young Palestinian looks at the waters of Tripoli's harbor. The PLO returned to Lebanon in early 1983. Arafat's supporters made Tripoli their new stronghold until they were driven from the city by PLO rebels and Syrian forces near the end of November.

A young Arafat supporter mans his position overlooking the Baddawi refugee camp, outside the northern Lebanese city of Tripoli, where fierce fighting between Arafat loyalists and dissident PLO members took place in November 1983. Arafat and his supporters were once again forced to leave Lebanon.

the world, and many Israelis criticized their government, particularly defense minister Ariel Sharon, for allowing it to happen. Public opinion in some parts of the world swung toward the PLO, who now cultivated the image of valiant underdogs pitted against a heartless aggressor.

The PLO was determined not to give up its operations in Lebanon. It needed a base from which to continue harassing Israel. Jordan was closed to it, and Syria was unfriendly. Lebanon was the only place left. Soon after Arafat arrived in Tunis, fedayeen began returning to Lebanon. Arafat even went so far as to set up a field office in the Baddawi refugee camp outside the Lebanese city of Tripoli, but Assad encouraged some PLO officials to believe that Arafat was no longer strongly committed to the goal of an independent Palestine and that he might agree to share power with Hussein. Alarmed at this possibility and disgusted with Arafat's increased willingness to negotiate a political solution to the Palestinian problem and with his retreat from Beirut, PLO dissidents rebelled in May 1983. Led by Sa'id Mousa, Arafat's former deputy chief of operations, rebel fedayeen in Lebanon's Bekaa Valley attacked PLO troops who remained loyal to Arafat. As the revolt spread, Syria sent tanks and troops into Lebanon to support the rebels.

By July the rebels held most of the Bekaa Valley. Arafat went to Damascus, to negotiate with Assad, who refused to see him and ordered him out of the country. This was a serious insult that damaged

Arafat's prestige in the Arab world, but it did not shake the loyalty of his followers. Groups of supporters demonstrated in the refugee camps outside Tripoli. Rebels fired on one such rally, killing 25 loyalists.

By November Arafat was on the run. He evacuated his headquarters in the Baddawi refugee camp hours before it was captured by Ahmed Jabril of the Popular Front for the Liberation of Palestine — General Command, who announced, "Arafat is finished. He has no alternative but to turn himself in to the revolution inside the PLO so he may receive the punishment he deserves." Unwilling to surrender, Arafat and his supporters endured another siege, this time in Tripoli, before once again fleeing Lebanon for Tunis.

Before he left Tripoli, Arafat managed to arrange an exchange of 6 Israeli prisoners for 4,700 Palestinian captives. It was the first prisoner exchange to which Israel had ever agreed. Many Israelis disapproved, saying that the terms were greatly unfair to Israel, but as he boarded a Greek ship bound from Tripoli to Tunis Arafat savored it as a small victory. In Tunis he would try for the second time in little more than a year to patch up his battered reputation and rebuild his organization.

Palestinian prisoners released by Israel rejoice as they board a UN ship bound for Algeria. Shortly before leaving Tripoli in November 1983, Arafat arranged the exchange of 6 Israeli prisoners for more than 4,500 Palestinians detained by Israel. Most had been captured during the Israeli invasion of Lebanon.

7

Today and Tomorrow

Perhaps it was his baraka that enabled Arafat to survive the rebellion within the PLO. While the world press speculated about his downfall after his flight from Tripoli, the PLO leader quietly began to forge new alliances.

On his way from Tripoli to Tunis he stopped in Egypt for a meeting with Hosni Mubarak, who had become president of Egypt after Sadat was assassinated in 1981. The move shocked both Arafat's supporters and his enemies because Arabs of all countries had been hostile to Egypt ever since Sadat's peace agreement with Israel. Many Arabs felt that Arafat's friendliness toward Mubarak would mark the end of his leadership of the PLO, but Arafat's senior colleagues in the PLO stood by him and called on other Arab nations to resume relations with Egypt.

The visit to Egypt gave Arafat one ally. He soon began building another surprising alliance, this time with King Hussein of Jordan. In early 1984 Hussein and Arafat agreed that they would have to work together to accomplish anything on behalf of the West Bank Palestinians. In a gesture of support for Arafat, Hussein invited the Palestine National Council to hold its annual meeting in Amman.

Egypt's welcome for the head of the murderous PLO is a severe blow to the peace process . . . the existence and the activities of the PLO contradicts peace. . . . The ultimate disappearance of this organization is a prerequisite for the achievement of peace and stability in this region.
—official Israeli statement after the reconciliation between Arafat and President Hosni Mubarak of Egypt, 1983

Palestinian boys wave the outlawed Palestinian flag in a camp in the Gaza Strip in April 1985. Behind them are the ruins of a house destroyed by the Israeli authorities, who suspected one of its occupants of being involved in an attack on an Israeli soldier the previous day.

101

Arafat accepted the invitation, and the PLO returned to Jordan for the first time in 14 years. The event was regarded as a triumph for Arafat, and he was reelected to the chairmanship of the PLO, ending Assad's attempts to gain control of the organization. The rebellion in the ranks withered and died. Many of the rebel fedayeen left the Bekaa Valley and rejoined Arafat's troops. The rebel leaders retired to Syria.

Arafat's reconciliation with Hussein was short lived; within a year the Jordanian king broke off relations with Arafat and closed down Fatah's office in Amman. Relations with the Tunisians were also shaky. After a 1985 raid in which Israeli warplanes bombed PLO headquarters in Tunis, the Tunisians made it clear that the PLO should move elsewhere. But no other nation was willing to take in the PLO, one of whose officials admitted to a reporter that "where to sleep is becoming a problem."

Arafat met with Jordan's King Hussein in April 1983. Two years later Arafat and Hussein presented a joint peace proposal based on Israel's withdrawal to its pre-1967 borders.

Meanwhile, Israeli settlers continued to build homesteads and towns in the West Bank, and slightly more than half the Israeli public favored the annexation of the West Bank and Gaza. While that debate proceeded, the Palestinian refugee population continued to swell. By the late 1980s, 61 camps in the occupied territories, Syria, Jordan, and Lebanon were home to nearly 2 million Palestinian refugees, while the total Palestinian population living in Israel and elsewhere in the world approached 5 million.

In January 1987, Hussein and Arafat reconciled their differences once again — the prelude to an astonishing series of events. In April, at a meeting in Algeria of the Palestine National Council (PNC), the Palestinians' "parliament-in-exile," Arafat was overwhelmingly affirmed as the leader of the Palestinian people by all the major constituent groups — including the PFLP and the PDFLP, which had been trying to overthrow him not long before. Having completed his improbable comeback to a position of undisputed leadership, Arafat began a series of secret talks with prominent Israelis, some of them members of the Israeli parliament, aimed at the eventual establishment of a dialogue between the PLO and

Israel. "I appeal with an open heart to the people of Israel," Arafat told a reporter from an Israeli communist newspaper; "it is impossible to wipe out 5 million Palestinians, just as it is impossible to wipe out Israel." Despite Arafat's softening stance toward the Jewish state, the Israeli government continued to reject any possibility of negotiating with Arafat or the PLO.

In December 1987, while the secret talks were dragging on, there occurred a relatively minor incident that would have a profound effect on Israeli-Palestinian relations. In Gaza, an Israeli army vehicle collided with some civilian trucks, killing four Arabs. The incident sparked spontaneous protests that immediately took on an anti-occupation character and quickly spread to Arab communities in the West Bank. It was the beginning of the *intifada* (Arabic for uprising), in which groups of locally organized, stone-throwing Arab youths harassed IDF patrols, while merchants, laborers, and consumers

Arafat with Egyptian president Hosni Mubarak in Cairo in November 1985. During his visit Arafat issued a statement in which he condemned the use of terrorism and promised to punish any members of the PLO who violated this policy.

Israeli settlers build new houses on the West Bank in the late 1970s. Menachem Begin's government, which lasted from 1977 to 1983, was particularly active in encouraging Jewish settlement and vowed never to relinquish control over the occupied territories.

took part in strikes against the Israeli administration. The local organizers forbade the use of guns, bombs, or other lethal weapons against the Israelis, particularly after the occupation forces responded to the start of the intifada by killing several Arab youths; the organizers reasoned that the violent Israeli response would turn the tide of world opinion to the Palestinian cause.

In January 1988, supporters of the sizable Israeli peace movement staged protests against their government's handling of the intifada. In March, the U.S. government, perhaps spurred by public opinion polls indicating that the majority of Americans disapproved of Israel's response to the intifada,

stepped up pressure on Israel to stop using lethal force against civilians. The occupation forces switched to rubber and plastic bullets, but Arab fatalities continued to mount.

The PLO, which had played no part in the intifada, sought to make contact with the organizers so that it could take a leading role. Arafat assigned Abu Jihad the task of linking up with the organizers, but the Israelis learned of the plan. In April they sent a commando squad to Tunisia for a secret nighttime landing; the commandos broke into Abu Jihad's villa, killed three bodyguards, then machine-gunned the PLO commander as he sat in his study, leaving more than 70 slugs in his body. The Israeli government soon admitted that it had carried out the assassination.

An Israeli soldier fires rubber bullets at stone-throwing Arab youths during the *intifada*, the Palestinian uprising against Israel's occupation of the West Bank and Gaza. From late 1987 through April 1989, 430 Arabs and 21 Israelis were killed by Israeli forces, rioters, and Israeli and Arab vigilante groups.

But the Israeli operation failed to slow the momentum of the Palestinian cause. In June, King Hussein announced that Jordan had abandoned its claim to the West Bank and now considered the region to be Palestinian territory. On November 15, 1988, the PNC met in Algiers and declared the establishment of the Palestinian state. The PNC declaration called for Israel to withdraw from the West Bank and Gaza, yet it also renounced terrorism and affirmed Israel's right to exist. For the first time ever, the PLO had officially endorsed a "two-state" solution to the Israeli-Palestinian conflict. The next day, 27 countries recognized the nation of Palestine.

Arafat was scheduled to address the UN in New York in December 1988, but the United States refused to grant an entry visa to the PLO leader, whose recent pledges to seek a peaceful solution, the U.S. government stated, could not be believed. Meanwhile, Arafat met with five liberal American Jewish leaders in Sweden. After two days of talks, the Jewish leaders told reporters that they believed Arafat and endorsed his efforts. Arafat, asked repeatedly by reporters whether he and the Palestinian movement truly accepted Israel's right to exist, answered, "The PNC accepted two states, a Palestinian state and a Jewish state, Israel. Is that clear enough?"

Arafat addresses the UN in Geneva, Switzerland, in December 1988, one month after he and the Palestine National Council affirmed Israel's right to exist, renounced terrorism, and declared the establishment of the Palestinian state. Despite the PLO's recognition of Israel, the United States refused to allow Arafat to address the UN in New York; consequently, the session was held in Switzerland.

Finally, on December 13, Arafat addressed a special session of the United Nations held in Geneva, Switzerland. He strode to the lectern to give his speech, but unlike his 1974 appearance, he wore no pistol holster. Urging the Israelis to pledge themselves to negotiations, Arafat said to the world body, "I ask the leaders of Israel to come here, under the sponsorship of the United Nations, so we can forge peace." The next day the U.S. government issued a statement that, in effect, endorsed Arafat's call for settlement talks to begin.

As 1989 began, an increasingly isolated Israel remained steadfast in its refusal to negotiate with the PLO. A top Israeli cabinet minister went on record as saying there would be no peace in the Middle East as long as Arafat "runs around alive," a statement clarified by an Israeli spokesman as reflecting the minister's "personal opinion that Mr. Arafat should be killed." Meanwhile, the intifada raged on. By April 1989, 430 Palestinians had been killed by Israeli forces, Jewish vigilante groups, and other Palestinians; 21 Israeli soldiers and civilians had been killed, most of them by Palestinians.

No one knows what the future holds for the Palestinians, the Israelis, or for Arafat himself. But whatever happens, he will be remembered as a controversial and passionately committed man who used all possible means — warlike and peaceful — to realize his people's long-held dream of self-determination.

Few modern historical figures have provoked reactions as intense as Yasir Arafat has. His success in building the Palestine liberation movement suggests that no peace will come to the Middle East until Palestinian self-determination is a reality.

Further Reading

Antonius, George. *Arab Awakening*. New York: Gordon Press, 1976.

Bill, James, and Carl Leiden. *The Middle East: Politics and Power*. Boston: Allyn & Bacon, 1974.

Carroll, Raymond. *Palestine Question*. New York: Franklin Watts, 1983.

Churchill, Winston S., and Randolph S. Churchill. *The Six Day War*. London: Heinemann, 1967.

Goldschmidt, Arthur, Jr. *A Concise History of the Middle East*. Boulder, CO: Westview, 1979.

Gordon, Matthew. *Ayatollah Khomeini*. New York: Chelsea House, 1987.

———. *The Gemayels*. New York: Chelsea House, 1988.

Harkabi, Yehoshafat. *Arab Attitudes to Israel*. New Brunswick, NJ: Transaction Books, 1974.

Hart, Alan. *Arafat*. Topsfield, MA: Salem House, 1984.

Hudson, Michael. *Arab Politics: The Search for Legitimacy*. New Haven: Yale University Press, 1977.

Kiernan, Thomas. *The Man and the Myth: Arafat*. New York: Norton, 1976.

Kirisci, Kemal. *The PLO and World Politics*. New York: St. Martin's Press, 1986.

Laqueur, Walter, and Barry Rubin, eds. *The Israel-Arab Reader*. New York: Penguin Books, 1975.

Matusky, Gregory, and John P. Hayes. *King Hussein*. New York: Chelsea House, 1987.

Miller, Aron David. *The PLO and the Politics of Survival*. New York: Praeger, 1983.

Mishal, Shaul. *The PLO Under Arafat: Between Gun and Olive Branch*. New Haven: Yale University Press, 1986.

Petran, Tabitha. *The Struggle Over Lebanon*. New York: Monthly Review Press, 1987.

Shipler, David K. *Arab and Jew: Wounded Spirits in a Promised Land*. New York: Times Books, 1986.

Sobel, Lester A., ed. *Palestinian Impasse: Arab Guerillas & International Terror*. New York: Facts on File, 1977.

Stefoff, Rebecca. *West Bank/Gaza Strip*. New York: Chelsea House, 1988.

Taylor, Alan R. *Arab Balance of Power*. Syracuse, NY: Syracuse University Press, 1982.

Chronology

Aug. 24, 1929	Born Rahman Abdul Rauf Arafat al-Qudwa al-Husseini in Cairo, Egypt
Nov. 29, 1947	United Nations votes to partition Palestine
May 1948	Independent state of Israel proclaimed; neighboring Arab states attack
July 1952	Arafat founds Palestinian Student Federation (PSF) Gamal Abdel Nasser overthrows Egyptian monarchy
1953	Arafat voted out of the PSF; founds General Union of Palestinian Students (GUPS)
July 1956	Member of Egyptian army during Suez crisis
1957	Founds al-Fatah movement in Kuwait
Jan. 18, 1964	Establishment of Palestinian Liberation Organization (PLO)
July 9, 1967	Israel defeats Jordan, Syria, and Egypt in the Six-Day War
March 21, 1968	Arafat leads Fatah fighters in the Battle of Karameh
1969	Elected chairman of the PLO
Sept. 1972	Members of PLO faction Black September take Israeli athletes hostage at the Olympic Games in Munich, West Germany; nine athletes killed
Feb. 1973	Arafat becomes head of PLO political department
Oct. 1973	October, or Yom Kippur, War between Israel and Egypt, Syria and Iraq
Nov. 1974	Arafat addresses the United Nations General Assembly in New York City
June–Aug. 1982	Israel invades Lebanon in attempt to wipe out PLO bases there; Arafat and PLO forced to evacuate to Greece, Tunisia, and Yemen
Sept. 1982	Massacre of Palestinians in Sabra and Shatila refugee camps by Lebanese Christians
1983	Revolt by PLO rebels against Arafat
1984	Arafat reelected chairman of the PLO
1985	Israel rejects peace proposal offered by Arafat and Jordan's king Hussein; Israeli planes bomb PLO headquarters in Tunis
1987	Arafat reelected by Palestine National Council (PNC); intifada begins in Gaza and West Bank in December
1988	Israeli commandos assassinate Abu Jihad in Tunisia (April); Jordan abandons its claim on West Bank (June); PNC declares establishment of Palestinian state, renounces terrorism, affirms Israel's right to exist (Nov.); Arafat addresses UN in Geneva (Dec.)
1989	Israel continues to reject talks with PLO; intifada continues, with a total of 430 Arabs and 21 Israelis dead by April

Index

Rebecca Stefoff holds a Ph.D. in English from the University of Pennsylvania, where she taught from 1974 to 1977. The author of works of fiction and non-fiction, she currently serves as editorial director of the Chelsea House series PLACES AND PEOPLES OF THE WORLD, to which she has contributed the volume entitled *West Bank/Gaza Strip*. She is also the author of *King Faisal* in the Chelsea House series WORLD LEADERS PAST & PRESENT.

Arthur M. Schlesinger, jr., taught history at Harvard for many years and is currently Albert Schweitzer Professor of the Humanities at City University of New York. He is the author of numerous highly praised works in American history and has twice been awarded the Pulitzer Prize. He served in the White House as special assistant to Presidents Kennedy and Johnson.